THE LOST TRIBE IN THE MIRROR

TO HOOSTIE,

Thanks for your signing
support,

regards,

Bill

THE LOST TRIBE IN THE MIRROR
Four Playwrights of Northern Ireland

PHILIP JOHNSTON

LAGAN PRESS
BELFAST
2009

Published by
Lagan Press
Unit 45
Westlink Enterprise Centre
30-50 Distillery Street
Beflast BT12 5BJ
e-mail: lagan-press@e-books.org.uk
web: lagan-press.org.uk

ISBN: 978 1 904652 47 2 (pbk)
978 1 904652 64 9 (hbk)
Author: Johnston, Philip
Title: The Lost Tribe in the Mirror
Four Playwrights of Northern Ireland
2009

Set in Palatino

for my father
Alexander Johnston

Acknowledgements

To Jim Hurt, with gratitude and admiration, Robert Graves, Nancy Blake, Peter Davis, Wanda Nettl, Sam McCready, Marie Jones, Ophelia Byrne, Leslie Bruce, Joan Murray, Alexander Murray, the Linen Hall Library, Belfast, the Central Library, Belfast, the BBC archives at Cultra, the Stewart Parker Trust and the University of Illinois Library at Urbana-Champaign.

Photographic Acknowledgements

The publishers would wish to thank the following for their permission reprint the photographs in this book: Chris Hill Photography for various production shots; the Linen Hall Library, Belfast, where many of the photographs are archived; and the Sam Thompson Archive housed at the Central Library, Belfast.

CONTENTS

Introduction   13

CHAPTER ONE
The Ulster Literary Theatre
Finding a Stage for Ulster Drama   21

CHAPTER TWO
Sam Thompson
The Naturalistic Image in the Mirror   29

CHAPTER THREE
Stewart Parker
Theories and Early Experiments   49

CHAPTER FOUR
Three Plays for Ireland   119

CHAPTER FIVE
Gary Mitchell
Refracting the Mirror   159

CHAPTER SIX
Marie Jones
Refiguring the Theatrical Landscape   185

Conclusion   205

Works Cited
Index

INTRODUCTION

In his introduction to a 1970 reissue of the Belfast playwright Sam Thompson's landmark play *Over the Bridge*, the younger Northern Irish playwright, Stewart Parker, wrote of seeing the first production in 1960: "We were like members of a lost tribe thrust before a mirror for the first time, scared and yet delighted by our own images, sensing even then that they were much more than a mere reflection. And the mirror was no missionary trinket, but the work of a dues-paying member of the tribe, a man with the plain Prod name of Sam Thompson." (Allen, 1987)

Northern Ireland did not see its reflection for the first time in *Over the Bridge* as a long tradition of Northern Irish drama had preceded it. Parker's words capture both the shock of the new in Thompson's brave work and the distinctive nature of its audience—an audience perceived in almost anthropological terms as atavistic, and outside the main tide of modernity, a 'Lost Tribe' both frightened and exhilarated to glimpse its collective face in the playwright-missionary's dramatic mirror. Parker's words recall not only the anthropological texts, but a dramatic one as well, Hamlet's injunction to the players to "hold the mirror up to nature", to "show the very age and body of the time his form and pressure" and M.H. Abrams' distinction between the 'mirror and the lamp' with art as a neutral reflector of reality, art as vision, the portrayal of possibilities as well as realities and much more than a mere reflection.

My book examines the work of four representative Northern Irish playwrights: Sam Thompson (1916-1965) and Stewart Parker (1941-1998), from the first wave of modern Northern Irish drama, and Gary Mitchell (1965-) and Marie Jones (1951-) from the second, as both mirrors and lamps held up to their Northern Irish audiences. These playwrights (and others who might have been included) are notable not only for their originality and technical skills but also as special and perhaps extreme examples of theatre's social function. 'The Lost Tribe' to whom they have addressed their plays is an audience split by seemingly intractable divisions: between Catholic and Protestant, Irish and British, centrifugal and centripetal. These divisions that are so far from being theoretical that their plays have often been performed under conditions that approximate a civil war with the sound of bombs and bullets penetrating theatres. All four playwrights have conceived (perhaps of necessity) of their work as socially committed, as interventions (direct or indirect) in the urgent issues of their time and place, as both mirrors (telling the truth about their part of the world) and lamps (illuminating a path forward).

All four playwrights are Protestant (in the special, cultural sense in which that word is used in Northern Ireland) and thus speak from the majority position (demographically) in Northern Ireland. But none is sectarian (again in the Northern Irish sense). All attempt to hold mirrors (and lamps) up to the whole society. What those theatrical mirrors and lamps are— the theatrical means by which the four playwrights have attempted both to reflect and to illuminate their culture—is the subject of this book.

The background to theatre in Northern Ireland is examined in Chapter One, 'The Ulster Literary Theatre: Finding a Stage for Ulster Drama' in the works of the founding Ulster playwrights.

In Chapter Two, 'Sam Thompson: The Naturalistic Image in the Mirror', the focus is the political and social tragedy in Thompson's first major play for the theatre *Over the Bridge* which marks a watershed in the revival of Northern Irish theatre. Thompson sought explanations for the basic insecurities of the Protestant working class, especially the exploitation of their ignorance and bigotry. The play was refused by the theatre management as it was determined that it would "affront the religious or political beliefs or sensibilities of the man in the street of any denomination or class in the community, and ... would give rise to sectarian or political controversy of an extreme nature". (Bell, 92)

Fifty-three years before *Over the Bridge* was performed, Gerald MacNamara's *Suzanne and the Sovereigns* (1907) had been considered 'risky material' in its representation of King William of Orange. Little seemed to have changed in 1960 as Thompson's 'risky' exposure of sectarianism at the Harland & Wolff shipyard in Belfast and inequality between Catholic and Protestant workers led the authorities to withdraw the play. In his naturalistic play Thompson discovered, as had Ibsen, that no dramatist lives through anything in isolation. What he lives through, his countrymen live through with him." (*Ibid*. 94)

Stewart Parker, like Thompson, voiced his concerns for a fractured society in which the playwright should play an active, guiding role. Parker's work was concerned with recurring themes of violence and reconciliation in Northern Irish drama. He saw *Over the Bridge* in 1960 and later wrote about the first night of the play and the indelible effect it had on his future career as a playwright. In Chapter Three, 'Stewart Parker: Theories and Early Experiments', Parker's early life and background in east Belfast, and its influence on his writing, is explored. His formative years at Sullivan Upper School and at Queen's University in Belfast, where he was part of a seminal literary group, led to his participation in the Drama Society as a director, writer and actor. At Queen's University Belfast he also founded the New Stage Club with the playwright Bill Morrison in 1963.

Parker's writings on theatre are central to the dramatic tradition in Northern Ireland. Thrust before the mirror of violence, Parker reflected, dispassionately, the hopelessness of the times, but he also shed light on imponderables, as he believed that things could improve if Northern Irish problems could be viewed objectively, and with a 'cool passion'. Parker's debt to major twentieth century theorists, including Brecht and Huizinga, are explored in this chapter as well as his own major explorations in 'Dramatis Personae', 'State of Play', 'Me and Jim' and other essays and articles on drama and theatre.

Living in the United States in the 1960s Parker was involved in the Civil Rights movement. In the theatre he saw many new experiments in African-American theatre, particularly the work of Amiri Baraka, who became a leader of the black arts revolutionary movement, viewing theatre as a weapon in the struggle for black liberation. Many of his plays dramatise social and racial problems in expressive forms and with unnerving frankness. Through reading Baraka's plays *Dutchman* (1964) and *Slave Ship* (1969) Parker could see how Baraka, and others, tried to invent a kind of play not based on western theatrical forms, like the Ibsenite problem play, but plays representing a new kind of social freedom. *Spokesong* was his first major breakthrough based not on an ordinary plot but on a central metaphor, the bicycle, in which traditional plot elements, when they are used, are used ironically, tongue in cheek.

Under the influence of Bertolt Brecht, Parker experimented with plays that steered away from illusion and likewise through his reading of Johan Huizinga he also restored 'playing' back into his plays. I will discuss: *The Iceberg* (1974), *Spokesong* (1975), *Catchpenny Twist* (1977), *Kingdom Come* (1977), *Nightshade* (1980), *Pratt's Fall* (1981) and the six-part television series *Lost Belongings* (1987). *Three Plays for Ireland*: *Northern Star* (1984), *Heavenly Bodies* (1986), *Pentecost* (1987) were published as a trilogy and represent the masterworks of a major twentieth-century Irish dramatist. The trilogy could be seen as building around a single, recurring metaphor: Irish history is like the theatre.

Like most playwrights from Northern Ireland, Parker's background frequently surfaces in his plays and nowhere more so than in *Three Plays for Ireland* which are discussed in Chapter Four. When dealing with a sadly foreshortened career like Stewart Parker's, the temptation is to concentrate on the work lost rather than the work achieved. The honesty, riskiness and excellence of his plays do heighten the sense of loss over the Irish epic Parker planned in collaboration with Trevor Nunn, or the nineteenth-century Irish western set in Donegal and Connaught or all the other projects, for that matter, that can only be imperfectly imagined. (Harris, 228)

Contemporary Northern Irish drama is represented in Chapter Five: 'Gary Mitchell: Refracting the Mirror'. Gary Mitchell writes because he believes that it is important that the world does not see only one side of life in Northern Ireland. The Protestant population has been misrepresented in the world by one-sided media reports, according to Mitchell, that have placed Protestantism under close scrutiny as never before. Mitchell uncovers painful truths within the Protestant community as his work reflects the present trend of introspection and shifting circumstances in contemporary Northern Ireland.

Ulster Protestant society has come under increasing strain as the political landscape has changed dramatically over the past decade. Mitchell's plays are unequivocal in presenting an unabashedly working-class Ulster Protestant perspective, a view rarely seen on stage. Mitchell takes a critical view of the Unionist establishment as he draws on the dissenting tradition of Protestantism which aligns him with many of the first dramatists of the Ulster Literary Theatre. Divided families, in Mitchell's persuasive view, are a metaphor for a divided community; he is adamant that his plays do not drown in 'localism' and states that they have 'universal relevance'. The plays examined in this chapter include: *In a Little World of Our Own* (1997), *As the Beast Sleeps* (1998), *Tearing the Loom* (1998) and *Marching On* (2000).

Marie Jones has been one of several women playwrights who have been struggling for representation in Irish theatre. Her work is examined in Chapter 6: 'Marie Jones: Refiguring the Theatrical Landscape'. The formation of Charabanc Theatre Company in 1983, by five unemployed Belfast actresses, marks the beginning of Jones' writing career as she sought to 'dig out' Belfast's lesser-known dramas. Jones' flexible talent, like that of Stewart Parker, is evident in her plays as she makes her own distinctive contribution to the fine Irish art of storytelling.

Jones was writer in residence and founding member of the Charabanc Theatre Company in Belfast from 1983 to 1990 during which time she wrote ten plays that toured extensively in Ireland, Britain and the United States. She has continued to write and produce her own work as well as adaptations of European classics. Jones does not regard herself as a feminist playwright but her inclusion in many critical studies of Irish women writers has placed her in that group. In Chapter 6, I will discuss *Lay Up Your Ends*, *Somewhere Over the Balcony*, *The Hamster Wheel*, *A Night in November*, and her most recent substantial work *Stones in His Pockets* as major contributions to theatre in Northern Ireland.

CHAPTER ONE

The Ulster Literary Theatre
Finding a Stage for Ulster Drama

A brief survey of Ulster theatre from the founding of the Ulster Literary Theatre (ULT) reveals that potential existed for a new type of committed drama in Ulster from the end of the nineteenth century. The ULT was founded in November 1902, in Belfast, and in 1904 two productions were written, acted and produced by the company in Ulster. Members of the ULT were openly critical of the Abbey Theatre in Dublin and its representation of Irish theatre that they believed excluded Ulster drama. The Ulster playwrights hoped to forge a regional and national identity but were criticised by the Abbey for their satiric levity in dealing with serious topics. In 1915 the ULT became the Ulster Theatre.

Uladh (Ulster) was the short-lived literary journal in which the Ulster playwrights announced their intention of writing their own plays, which they stated would be "more satiric than poetic" in answer to the poetic mysticism in the south of Ireland. The ULT proclaimed that it was non-sectarian and non-political and was concerned with fostering a distinctly Ulster branch of the Irish Literary Theatre (ILT). In the first publication of *Uladh*, the ULT stated: "We have not striven to erect a barrier between Ulster and the rest of Ireland; but we aim at building a citadel in

Ulster for Irish thought and art achievements such as exist in Dublin." (*Uladh*, 1905) The founders also believed that drama in Ulster had a much more cosmopolitan role to play and looked to other Europeans, Scandinavians and beyond to the Elizabethans and the Greeks: "While any other provocation would serve, we may as well use that which the Greeks, the Elizabethans and the contemporaries of Molière, and the Norway of Ibsen have utilised to such excellent purposes. So we intend to strike a keynote through our Theatre, where our own plays will be produced, and to let that discover our pathway for us and voice those aims and hopes and hatreds and loves best expressed that way." (*Samhain*, 1904)

The Ulster playwrights often experienced a sense of cultural inferiority, that continued even after the division of Ireland into two separate states, as they believed their cultural achievements had been sidelined and undervalued. This was reflected in cultural embarrassment which took two forms: the straightforward one of critical neglect, and the more damaging one whereby deep embarrassment calls for critical justification. "The plays had a sense of 'localism' and were often deficient in universal relevance which was manifested in imaginative moral impoverishment, a sense of 'clay feet' in which the archaic and outdated values of a rural ethos, or defunct social environment, give to them the patronising attribute of sociological but not artistic significance." (Smyth, 1993)

Northern Ireland was staunchly Unionist and resisted any movement associated with Celtic Mysticism, which it believed would lead to Irish Independence and Republicanism. In answer to the growing nationalist sentiment amongst the Dublin theatre community, the Ulster playwrights asserted that theatre in Ulster should maintain its own qualities that were distinctive from the other Irish provinces. The ULT's understanding of 'regionalism' is critical in two senses: its members recognised the critical differences between the four provinces of Ireland to be one of the nation's greatest strengths but they were critical of those regional factors, particularly Orangeism, as it prevented Ulster from playing its full role in the formation of a new nation. The ULT actively promoted a regional nationalism, a way of imagining a nation's strength and integrity in terms of its regional diversity, rather than a false homogeneity. (Lyons, 35-36)

The four editions of *Uladh* reiterated the need for truth and soul-searching to find the identity and culture of the Ulster population and its history, in times of peace and conflict. The essential nature of theatre, and local temperament, were the objectives of the Ulster playwrights at the turn of the century: "Exactly what the local temperament and artistic aptitude are, *Uladh* wants to discuss. *Uladh* would also influence them, direct and inform them, and as the theatre is the most essential of all art activities, and a sure test of a people's emotional and intellectual vitality, *Uladh* starts out as the organ of the theatre." (*Samhain*, 1904)

There was little encouragement from the Irish Literary Theatre in support of the Ulster dramatists. W.B. Yeats was hostile toward the ULT, refusing it permission to perform *Cathleen Ni Houlihan*, reminding the Ulster playwrights not to regard the ULT as the Northern branch of the Irish Literary Theatre. Bulmer Hobson and David Parkhill, founder members of the ULT, wished "to spread the ideas and principles of Wolfe Tone and the United Irishmen" (Bell, 2). They did not succeed in directing the theatre as a vehicle for propaganda, but they did, with the help of Maud Gonne, manage to persuade Yeats to allow the company to perform *Cathleen Ni Houlihan* in November 1902. The other play performed was *The Racing Lug* by James Cousins, a poet, playwright and teacher, born in Belfast, who moved to Dublin in 1897, where he received constant discouragement from W.B. Yeats.

Many Ulster writers had a tendency to hide under pseudonyms: Lewis Purcell (David Parkhill, 1880-1941), Rutherford Mayne (Sam Waddell, 1878-1967) and Gerald MacNamara (Harry C. Morrow 1865-1938) are seminal playwrights from the fledgling years of the ULT. It was evident during the first season of the ULT that the company could present work that was satiric, historic and political. Lewis Purcell's *The Reformers* (1904) was a satire on municipal robbery while Bulmer Hobson's *Brian of Banba* (1904) incorporated elements of Irish mythology. *Brian of Banba* had been published in the *United Irishman* in 1902 and was a forerunner of the plays of quality that were written by Ulster playwrights.

The first productions were accompanied by bombast in *Uladh*: "There is a strong undercurrent of culture in the North, and this we will endeavour to tap, and, if possible, turn into native channels ... We may roll the stone that has been pushed by others. Then the heroes of the north will ride forth again, at present they only sleep within the caverns of dark prejudice and ignorance and distrust." (*Samhain*, 1904) Dissension was also emerging within the ranks of the ULT concerning political allegiance and Ulster's Irishness.

Contrasts between the work written and produced by the ULT and the work of the ILT in Dublin filled the pages of *Uladh*. Bulmer Hobson's *Brian of Banba* was compared with the work of W.B. Yeats: "If in *Brian of Banba* the words do not 'sing and shine' as in *The King's Threshold*, if Mr. Hobson's figures have not the austere simplicity and magic appeal of Mr. Yeats' creations, yet he has drawn his inspiration from the same wells, and there is in his work something at once elemental and significant, beauty touched with strangeness." (Bell, 14)

Lewis Purcell's *The Enthusiast* (1905) was produced in the Clarence Place Hall in Belfast and is an important work in the Ulster theatre movement. The play begins a long tradition of plays in Ulster concerning agrarian rights and the political and religious divisions that created a physical barrier between the citizens of Ulster. *The Enthusiast* is concerned with the Home Movement Reformists, who are in opposition to the Unionist supporters, and with solutions to agrarian reforms without offending the opposing political and religious ideologies in the farming community. Forrest Reid (1875-1948), the Belfast novelist, said the play was "effective in its dramatic power and insight, in humour, in freshness, in originality, [and] is infinitely superior to any modern play that I have ever seen performed in Belfast. *The Enthusiast* is in short a little work of art and worth a hundred of the productions of the Pineros and Joneses we are so frequently asked to applaud today." (Mengel, 52)

Suzanne and the Sovereigns (1907) by Gerald MacNamara was a major success for the ULT. Rutherford Mayne's comments on the performance highlight the 'risky material' that Morrow exposed to a volatile public. Morrow "had the audacity to make one of the principal characters of the play no less a personage than King William III of 'glorious, pious and immortal memory' ... The reason for William's advent in Ulster was given as due to the impassioned appeal of a deputation from Sandy Row to save the daughter of their local Grand Master from the unwelcome attentions of the Catholic King James." (Bell, 30) It was a miracle, according to local critics, that the theatre was not besieged by angry mobs protesting the sacred memory of their Protestant King. The theatre proved to be the only place where this subject matter could be exposed and the anticipated riot turned to success by the 'irresistible wit and humour' in the play. Theatre riots, and plays that provoke them, were often the concern of the Dublin and Belfast theatres.

Rutherford Mayne was one of the most important figures in the Ulster Theatre movement; his first play *The Turn of the Road* (1906) was premiered by the ULT. It is a 'country kitchen' drama dealing with tensions between labour and the arts. Whitford Kane (1881-1956) the Ulster actor, who later established himself in the United States in theatre and film, attended the first production of *The Turn of the Road*: "It is for my introduction to the Ulster Literary Theatre, and to Rutherford Mayne in particular, that I am indebted for finding myself. One evening during one of my summer vacations he took me to see his first play *The Turn of the Road*. This performance must have struck some national chord in me, for I went again the next night; after that I was asked to join a gathering at the Arts Club. I heard for the first time some of the beautiful folk songs and poems of my own country, and as I listened I realised how Irish I really was, and also how intensely Irish Ulster was, in spite of its many peculiar distinctions." (Killen, 7)

As nationalism waned in the ULT's agenda, playwrights began to place greater emphasis on social realism, with its traditions and growth, alongside the rest of Ireland. This early experimental phase in Ulster playwriting lasted for ten years when the ULT had been able to find its particular artistic and political commitment, according to the standards set by *Uladh*. Of the plays written during this period some merit special attention as they had a highly formative influence on the entire theatre movement in Ulster, forming the mould, of something that might be called the Ulster Play.

The Ulster Play found its fullest expression in Mayne's *The Drone* (1908). The production premiere was a success at the Abbey and encouraged the *Irish Times* critic Forrest Reid to write: "Dublin must look to its laurels, as in everything else, when Ulster makes up its mind to try. We may say without exaggeration that no more significant production has been seen in Dublin in our day. We seem to be on the verge of a revolution in dramatic art, and remarkably enough, it has been left to Ulster to lead the way." (Bell, 32) The journal *Sinn Féin* was equally laudatory in its review of the play: "*The Drone* is a masterpiece of comedy of life and manners, the finest of its kind that has ever been put on the Irish stage by Irish players." (*Ibid*, 33)

Rutherford Mayne acted in, and wrote, plays that unashamedly used Ulster dialect and dress. His later plays *Peter* (1930) and *Bridgehead* (1934) were successfully produced at the Abbey Theatre. Writing to Lennox Robinson, Yeats commented on *Peter*: "The play shows great capacity for managing the stage, for keeping it vivid and amusing, I think it will be a great success at the Abbey ... it is a godsend ... of course we accept the play for the Abbey with the greatest possible satisfaction." (Killen, 13)

In 1909 Mayne had joined the Irish Land Commission, and in 1911 he was sent to supervise the redistribution of land in the West of Ireland. He did not return to live in Ulster again, but his final play *Bridgehead* (1934) is an affirmation of his Ulster roots. The play was inspired by his work for the land commission: "When the history of Irish Theatre comes to be written a century hence *Bridgehead* may well occupy a place equal in importance to that of *The Playboy of the Western World*, since, like Synge's masterpiece, it is one of those plays which pointed the way." (Killen, 14-15) *Bridgehead* was awarded the Casement Prize for the best Irish play of 1933-34.

During the first decades of the twentieth century the ULT produced many successful playwrights but leaner years followed during the 1930s to the 1950s when Ireland had come to an uneasy peace as it accepted division, reluctantly, in the hope that re-unification could be achieved in the future. Between 1940 and 1960 a number of playwrights continued to sustain the Ulster drama. Harry S. Gibson contributed two successful works for the Ulster Group Theatre: *Bannister's Café* (1949) and *The Square Peg* (1950).

Sam Hanna Bell makes an arbitrary division of the early years of the ULT: 1904-1911, the years of promise; 1912-1920, the years of fruition; and 1920-1934, the years of decline. (Bell, 49) The division of Ireland into North and South in 1921 was a major catalyst in the decline of the ULT as the outbreak of civilian violence in Ulster forced many playwrights to move to the United States or Dublin. The idealism of the early decades of the century evolved into hardened cynicism that drove playwrights and the theatre away from politically contentious issues.

CHAPTER TWO

Sam Thompson
The Naturalistic Image in the Mirror

Stewart Parker described Sam Thompson as a member of the 'lost tribe' of Protestant frontier planters who came to Northern Ireland from Scotland in the mid-seventeenth century. Thompson (1916-1965) began his writing career in east Belfast and became a catalyst for dramatists in Northern Ireland. Writing about Northern Ireland's fractured culture, in which the polarities of Protestant and Catholic—Unionist and Nationalist—were on a constant collision course, became the focus of Thompson's life. The characters he recalled were those tragic people who were victimised by a deeply divided, male-dominated, sectarian society. As a pivotal figure in the development of modern Irish drama, Thompson presented an authentic urban voice on the stage in Belfast producing his play *Over the Bridge* (1960) in the face of hostility from the Unionist establishment, as an indictment of sectarianism in people's working lives.

Over the Bridge is a naturalistic representation of everyday contemporary life at the Belfast shipyard. Thompson approached his subject matter with brutal honesty as he examined nationalism, socialism and the privileges given to Protestant workers in the Belfast shipyard. He made bigotry, and its effects, the enslavement of prejudice, fear and economic dependence the leitmotif of his realistic drama. Without being bitter and vindictive, he reflects in his play the harshness of the environment: "Serious criticism of Ulster drama in the past has tended to dismiss this close realism as a form of parochialism which did not compare well with the mature products of an established British and Irish drama of realism ... It never seems to have occurred to these critics that the realism of the northern playwrights might have its own endemic laws, and refute comparison with the works of Shaw, Synge or O'Casey. They must have overlooked that 'realism' as a creative perspective, is largely, if not entirely, conditioned by the 'reality' it sets out to portray." (Mengel, 174)

There had been no sense of unified identity in Northern Ireland, either before or after the division of Ireland, and there was no mythology around which to construct a cultural nationalism as the drama in Northern Ireland was structured around conflicting identities and a fragmentation of culture. In writing *Over the Bridge*, Thompson's meticulous realism was based on his knowledge, general and specific, of the life and work of his community, rather than delving into the psychology of individuals. The play is concerned with presenting archetypes rather than heroic figures, and in this way Thompson stood firmly in the tradition of Ulster realism.

The industrial landscape of Belfast was the backdrop for Thompson's plays of the early 1960s, during which time he became a household name, and this was, by any standard, a rare accomplishment for a playwright and former shipyard worker. Thompson was gifted with eloquence and educated by his parents in a spirit which was non-sectarian and which brought him, in later life, to a compassionate understanding of Belfast's working population. He was a staunch believer in trade unionism and fought for the rights of his fellow workers. Parker highlighted the antagonism experienced by Thompson from the establishment: "During the Westminster election of 1964, when

Lord O'Neill of the Maine was still plain Captain (he later became Prime Minister) he made reference to 'a certain Mr. Sam Thompson whose past experience is, I gather, on producing works of fiction'. A lot of blood has since flowed under the bridge and it is a sarcasm to which posterity has not been kind. Bridges are a favorite Ulster metaphor. Bridge building between the communities has become the compulsory sport of our captains and our kings. The traditional sport of stirring up sectarian hatreds, however, continues to be played at times of stress like election campaigns, or when deciding upon a suitably provocative name for an actual steel and concrete bridge." (Parker 7, Introduction to *Over the Bridge*)

The experience of seeing *Over the Bridge* had a profound effect on Parker as he shared, with Thompson, an east Belfast background that influenced and informed much of his writing: "The Ballymacarrett district of Belfast was a good environment to come from if you wanted to be a writer; you struggled with the place because you were told you were British with an allegiance to a monarch and yet there was the feeling that you were Irish. If you managed to get through it there was a great advantage to draw from such a background, which enabled the playwright to write British as well as Irish characters." Going over the bridge was, as Parker states, another activity which demanded a degree of guts and integrity, which public life in Ireland had failed to cultivate, and one to which Thompson had dedicated his life: "He coaxed, commanded, persuaded and implored his mulish fellow-countrymen to make the journey. He wasn't a captain or a king but a shipyard painter and they listened to him ... they knew the reality of his fiction." (*Ibid* 7)

Early childhood memories would clearly play a pivotal role in Thompson's life and career as a painter in the Harland & Wolff shipyard and as a playwright. Life in Belfast during the 1920s and 1930s was grim for the working classes, both Catholic and Protestant. Thompson recalled going without shoes in the winter and bringing a penny to school each week in winter for the coal and gas fund. The children who failed to bring a penny were placed at the back of the classroom where it was cold. Thompson's father was a lamplighter and part-time sexton, which helped the family avoid the extremes of poverty.

Thompson remembered old men wandering about the wharves vainly watching boats come up the Belfast Lough in the hope they meant repair work. As a member of the National Council of Labour Colleges (a fact that he kept a secret from his staunchly Unionist parents) and as an active trade unionist, he also belonged to the Northern Ireland Labour party. An NCLC course took Thompson to France before the Second World War and a planned visit to Russia in 1939. All of these ventures were anomalous for an east Belfast Protestant whose allegiance should have focused on the Unionist Party and the Orange Order, which were fiercely opposed to connections with communism or Catholicism.

Thompson moved from job to job and spent eighteen months in Manchester during the war years before returning to Belfast where he worked on his own as an independent painting contractor. He was in his late thirties when he began to transmute his east Belfast experiences into drama. During this time, Sam Hanna Bell for the BBC in Belfast commissioned work for radio with a programme about Queen's Island on which Harland & Wolff had built its shipping empire.

After his marriage, Thompson moved to Craigmore Street, Belfast, which was close to the BBC. He discovered a local pub that was frequented by radio and television writers. One evening he was overheard by Sam Hanna Bell, a BBC talks producer, telling shipyard stories. Bell told him to write them down and invited him to help out on a radio feature about the shipyard called *The Island Men*. During the following years Bell was to produce six Thompson radio features.

His major works for the BBC include *Brush in Hand* (1956, in which he recalled his own apprenticeship in the Shipyard), *Tommy Baxter — Shop Steward* (1957), *The General Foreman* (1958)

and *The Long Back Street* (1958), an autobiographical account of
the street where he grew up in working-class Belfast. *We Built a
Ship* (1959) is an abandoned play about the gruelling work at
Harland & Wolff. His radio serial for the BBC, *The Fairmans*
(1959), was the network's most successful serial. The programme
was aimed at capturing the same type of audience that Joseph
Tomelty's *The McCooeys* reached during the 1950s.

Thompson's work was often compared to that of Tomelty but
fell short of the audience for Tomelty's work in which low
comedy and cheap melodrama had been paraded before them.
Tomelty was, however, a superb craftsman who was gifted with
a keen awareness of the wishes of the audience, whereas
Thompson's work depicted the everyday story of the Fairman
family and the problems of work, unemployment, migration,
homelessness, family coherence, old age and loneliness.

Working for BBC radio enabled Thompson to give up his job
at Harland & Wolff to become a full-time writer. Felicitous as this
success was, it does not in itself account for his becoming a
writer. All his life Sam Thompson had been half-consciously
storing material in his imagination while his body and mind met
the harsh demands of working-class life. His triumph was to
demonstrate that an act of writing is possible even from deep
down in the mines of what he nicknamed 'the Siberia of the arts'.
He was, according to Parker, "a bona fide prophet without so
much as an honorary degree and too controversial for the Belfast
cultural establishment". (*Ibid* 7)

Playwriting was a natural progression for Thompson, as he
possessed a skill for language, dialogue and plots centring on
east Belfast. The first play came out of his experience and was
based upon two incidents that played a pivotal role in his
subsequent development as a playwright. The first was one in
which, as a boy of six, he witnessed a man being beaten by a mob
and left for dead on Belfast's Castlereagh Road. The second
occurred when Italy invaded Abyssinia in 1935 and Protestant
mobs ran through the workshop of the shipyard to expel their

Catholic fellow workers. *Over the Bridge* is a powerful plea for moderation and communal peace, and focuses on a Protestant trade unionist who is killed trying to save a Roman Catholic worker from a rioting mob.

The opening scene establishes the environment, protagonists and themes around which the play develops:

RABBIE: (*Sings*) 'Lead kindly light. Amid the encircling gloom. Lead thou me on.' (*Warren Baxter silently opens the office door and stands watching.*)

RABBIE: (*To himself*): Perm two groups of four from six groups of four. Fifteen lines at tuppence a line. Half-crown staked. (*He sings*) 'The night is dark, and I am from home, Lead thou me on.'

BAXTER: Man, you're a bloody ould hypocrite, too. Rabbie. Singing hymns while you mark your football coupon in the firm's time.

RABBIE: (*startled*): For Pete's sake, you whistle before you come in, Baxter. Do you want to give me a heart attack?

BAXTER: Relax, Rabbie, relax.

RABBIE: I thought you were ould Fox.

BAXTER: No such luck. It's only the poor Shop Steward, here on official business—public doormat number one, for bosses and workmates alike.

RABBIE: Don't take yourself so seriously, Baxter. Better men than you have been Shop Stewards and survived it. Have you broke the news to him yet? (21)

Thompson creates an atmosphere around these characters that seems at first unspecified as he gives a number of apparently trivial and at the same time succinct social references. Trade unionism is high on the list of the shipyard agenda and is coupled with talk of the work of the Shop Steward. Rabbie, the older of the two men, warns Baxter to be careful in the presence of Mr. Fox, the Head Foreman. Baxter and Rabbie are not cardboard characters but real people with hopes, fears, passion and resignation, making *Over the Bridge* not an artfully orchestrated character drama but a drama of discussion in which individuals reflect upon the problems which determine their collective environment and life.

The environment asserts itself as the main protagonist in *Over the Bridge*, shaping the lives and ideas of the people who live in it. A strict hierarchy governs life in the shipyard and the relationships between the workers and the management are of as much consequence as the battles between the larger than life heroes in classical drama. According to Bertolt Brecht, this is the land, which is fortunate enough to need no heroes as the people living in it are exhibiting just as broad a range of human responses and emotions as the heroes of classical or bourgeois drama.

The evil effects of sectarianism were pervasive in Northern Ireland. The shipyard workers and their families found the basis of communal solidarity eroded and destroyed with the hopes and lives of those who wished to build on love, understanding and tolerance. *Over the Bridge* is a parable of stark and ferocious simplicity that Parker appropriately compared to the archetypal morality play *Everyman* in which extremes of human behaviour fight against one another in a tale that telescopes the entire misbegotten history of Northern Ireland sectarianism into one impressive incident.

Religion becomes the central focus in *Over the Bridge* when the light-hearted rapport of the first scene shifts to a more aggressive questioning of the trade union movement and its connection to sectarianism in the shipyard. Rabbie questions Warren about his trade union principles as Warren has taken over from his predecessor as the convener for Shop Stewards. His predecessor had not concerned himself about union matters and Rabbie states that he got the job "because he played the taig against the Prod". A heated discussion on sectarianism follows his statement:

> BAXTER: Exactly. And it'll be no different when I go for the job. The same bigoted prejudice will creep in again.

[35]

RABBIE: Are you saying that because your opposing nominee is a Derry man and a Catholic?

BAXTER: Correct. Seventy-five per cent of our members are Prods. They'll vote for me because I'm Prod. Except of course they have a better Prod than me in mind. (36)

Through the dialogue that follows, Thompson shows his skill in illustrating the general by describing the individual. Rabbie and Davy Mitchell come from the older generation while Baxter represents the younger and more direct generation. The discussion between these characters presents one of the central issues in the play, the conflict between the workers' movement and the shop stewards.

Sectarians are inward-looking and are gifted with an enormous capacity for discrediting and disregarding the physical reality outside of their own narrow frame of reference in their lack of unity and tolerance. Any attempt from the trade unionists to force the sectarians to justify themselves before their official meeting is pointless. The arrival of the arch bigot, Archie Kerr, who was played in the original production by Thompson, brings sectarian conflict into the open. There has been an explosion at the shipyard and rumour has spread that it is the work of the IRA. The assumption of the shipyard bigots is that any Catholic working in the shipyard must be suspect. Rabbie points out that Peter O'Boyle is the only Catholic member who had been nominated to his branch of the trade union and Baxter also reiterates that he was seconded to this position by 'two Prods':

RABBIE: [*agitatedly*]: If a man is elected on to the district committee and does a good job, I don't give a damn if he is Catholic or a Rumanian hemstitcher.

ARCHIE: Well, don't say I didn't warn you. When the time comes for a showdown we'll not only number the Popeheads as the enemies of Ulster, but we'll have to take into account mealy-mouthed Prods like you who aid and abet them. We're not standing for a Fenian like O'Boyle sitting on the district committee who takes his instructions from an illegal organisation or some ould black crow of a Jesuit. (40)

Archie Kerr is intent on destroying any attempt to make the trade union movement inclusive as he fosters loyalist intolerance that is irrational, primitive and governed by the narrow-minded principles of the Orange Lodge. The ensuing argument between Rabbie and Archie focuses on Archie's equating Catholicism with Communism in an irrational argument that combines half-truths. Although he is not the originator of the bigotry, which has festered for so long at the shipyard, his voice becomes the dominant one in the play in the cycle of retribution and violence.

Forms of collective self-righteousness from both Catholic and Protestant are as hopeless as sectarianism and its alignment with racism. Selfishness is explored in the character George Mitchell who has spent his working life at the shipyard securing work and working overtime at the expense of his fellow workers, for which the union fines him. In the first scenes of the play the hierarchy of the labour movement and the tense working environment that has created the history of the Belfast shipyard are established. Thompson is not dealing with the fates of individuals but rather with the historical development of an environment. The characters depicted may have a specific identity and characteristic features but they are really onstage because they represent aspects of the environment.

In scene three of Act 1: "It is evening of the same day, in the home of Davy Mitchell. His daughter, Marian, is humming as she irons a frock. She stops, alarmed, at the sound of an explosion in the distance. Then she walks over to the fireplace, lifts a poker and raps the wall with its handle. She returns to the ironing board still looking anxious. A moment later her next-door neighbour Martha White, Rabbie's wife, enters." (49) The two women do not work outside the home and their lives are governed by the availability of work for their husbands at the shipyard. Women are secondary characters in Thompson's work as they reflect the world outside. The sound of the explosion begins the unfolding drama:

> MARIAN: Father's always telling me that the pattern of all Belfast life is to be found in the shipyard. Does Rabbie believe that, Martha?
>
> MARTHA: Every word of it. Rabbie says that down there you get the two extremes, from the devout Christians to the fellows who would steal the Lord's Supper.
>
> MARIAN: In a town like Belfast, Martha, religion can be the cause of a lot of trouble.
>
> MARTHA: Not religion dear, but people who have made religion what it is ... Isn't it odd how they chop and change their interpretation of the scriptures all the time? I told Morgan's wife that in the fruit shop the other day when she invited me to one of her meetings. Maggie, says I, it would take a body to keep themselves well up to date with the sect you belong to, for if you ever missed one meeting, you'd become a heretic overnight. No, Marian, I'll stick to the established Church, they're longer in the business. (51)

The women warn, shelter, console and help each another in times of crisis. Local caring and affection can also turn on the renegade, with vengeance, as happens in the following scene as George Mitchell and his wife Nellie move up the social ladder to the salubrious suburbs, where insignificant status symbols raise them out of their original backgrounds. The social deprivations of the 1930s were in living memory and the well-being of the Protestant worker depended on the shipyard as Martha reminds us at her wedding: " ... but there I was, all dressed in white, thinking about the empty slipways in the shipyard, and the choir singing 'The Lord is my Shepherd, I shall not want'." (54)

The closing lines in Act 1 foreshadow the impending violence of Act 2:

> DAVY: There's nothing civilised about a mob, Warren, be it Protestant or Catholic. They can store their bigotry for a long time. Then they spew it out in violence. (*A grim silence settles in. The curtain falls.*) (64)

The shipyard is a reflection of twentieth-century politics in Northern Ireland. The conflict between Orangeism and liberalism for the allegiance of Ulster Protestants is over. Orangeism has won and the Ulster bosses have ensured the loyalty of the Protestant masses at the price of permanently maintaining discrimination and Protestant supremacy. Sixty years later, when some Unionist leaders were to contemplate dismantling some of the apparatus of the Orange state for the soundest of capitalist reasons, their followers would revolt. The Orange ideology, with its combination of Protestant supremacy and evangelical fervour, would assume a life of its own and defy its masters. (Farrell, 59)

This is reflected in mob rule at the shipyard where the management and the union leaders are no longer able to keep control:

FOX: Religion plays a hell of a part in the lives of the people in this country, for all the good it does them. Thirty Catholic workers in my department alone who are all union members, and what happens—they're chased out of their employment because someone raised the rumour that it was a time bomb that damaged that sub-station.

RABBIE: The union doesn't sanction mob law.

FOX: Then what the hell is it all about? Can't the union do something to protect its members in their employment? Isn't it their duty?

RABBIE: We can't control a mob. (67)

The unions were complicit in the the impending disaster as years of worker abuse and an illicit sanctioning of sectarianism by the management are a reflection of the outside political struggle lying at the heart of shipyard violence. Archie Kerr reports that a sectarian gang is about to descend on Fox's offices to ferret out Peter O'Boyle, who has been kept there by the management for his own safety, as Baxter looks out of the window to report on the violent crowd. This device serves to heighten the tension for the audience and to highlight the anonymity of the armed mob that is ready to attack O'Boyle as he confronts them. If he leaves quietly and goes home, his life would be spared but his rights as a worker would be subjugated to mob rule and his basic human rights taken from him. O'Boyle's decision to stay leads to a dramatic inevitability characteristic of heroic tragedy. The real hero in the play is, however, Davy Mitchell, who sacrifices his own life in trying to save O'Boyle.

The emotional turmoil and language is emphatic and urgent with invocations 'for Pete's sake' and 'by Christ'. In the final scene of Part 1 Thompson demonstrates the unconditional surrender of reason to the threat of advancing irrationalism. Rabbie's resigned "mobs don't reason" is an admission of defeat on behalf of the men in the office. Throughout the play his attitude is represented as a position deeply rooted in the history of Northern Irish society: "Davy's sacrifice should also not be seen as an isolated act but rather as an action of 'symbolic relevance' which reflects the faith and courage of all those men and women in Ulster who, over the years, have cried out against the perversion and vilification of the human image by bigoted sectarianism." (Mengel, 286)

The critics praised Thompson's work as the first of its kind to bring real-life workmen onto the stage without making them look out of place. There were other Ulster playwrights who had succeeded in presenting working-class characters on stage. But Thompson was the first playwright whose work reflected an absolute concurrence of experience and ideas. If the scenes in the play are taken in isolation, including those that are melodramatic, they have an epic quality. Thompson explains and demonstrates, on stage, the history and ritual of life in Protestant east Belfast.

An unwritten code of censorship was in place in Northern Ireland and although the authorities had not succeeded in banning Gerald McLarnon's *The Bonefire* (1958), the apparatus of Ulster unionism was firmly behind the decision to keep *Over the*

Bridge off the Belfast stage. It is difficult to imagine a man with Thompson's temperament taking on the establishment, which he did, forcefully. Other plays had delved deeply into the national consciousness where issues of poverty, religion and politics were brought to public attention: St John Ervine's *Mixed Marriage* (1911), Joseph Tomelty's *The End House* (1944), Carnduff's writings about the shipyard workers, *Songs from the Shipyard* (1924) and *Workers* (1932). The harrowing report in *Over the Bridge* from the heartland of sectarianism coupled with the potential for forming a new type of committed drama in Ulster was what the local people called 'dead on'. It had a genuineness with regard to language and an unwavering devotion to the discussion of the most central problems of the working population of Belfast, which distinguished it from the common run of plays in the tradition of Ulster realism.

Thompson's theme in *Over the Bridge* was prophetic as there would never be peace in Belfast until there was harmony and tranquility in the shipyard. The banning of the play was also intrinsically linked to the politics of Northern Ireland and the attempts by the Unionist party to replace the Prime Minister, Lord Brookeborough, with Terence O'Neill. In Belfast in the late 1950s, under Lord Brookeborough's rigid government, anyone critical of Unionism was silenced. "Lord Brookeborough was brought from the backwoods of County Fermanagh to defend Unionist bastions in the face of improved global communications and better articulated ideas on how post-war societies in Western Europe could be run without killing half the population in every generation." (Devlin, 1985)

What was happening in the theatre in Belfast had already been happening in London and Dublin. John Osborne's *Look Back in Anger* (1956) began a new era in British drama with the angry rhetoric of its protagonist directed in defence of the underprivileged. In Dublin, during the 1959 Festival, Alan Simpson, the manager of the Pike Theatre, had been charged in the Dublin High Court for producing Tennessee Williams' *The*

Rose Tattoo (1951). He was accused of the ridiculous charge of exhibiting obscenities on stage for profitable gain. "Behind the scenes, charging about like Don Quixote tilting at windmills was that arrogant old bigot (sic) Archbishop McQuaid, who also forced the Dublin Theatre Festival to proscribe Sean O'Casey's *The Drums of Father Ned* (1958) and the dramatised version of James Joyce's *Ulysses*." (*Ibid*)

Over the Bridge was aimed at exposing sectarianism and the directors of the Ulster Group Theatre finally rejected it. In his notes, Thompson describes the meeting with the director of the theatre who felt, along with many others, that the play could only lead to violence. After listening to broadcast of *The Long Back Street* at the home of Ritchie McKee, the Chairman of the BBC in Belfast, Thompson recollected: "When the programme ended McKee jumped to his feet and congratulated me on what he called a 'fine piece of writing'. But it wasn't long before we got down to *Over the Bridge*. I let him have his say ... he wanted the mob scene out and the language curtailed ... in his opinion the religious references in the play were blasphemous. Strangely enough I am now the proud possessor of two cuttings praising my play. They appeared in two religious papers, the *Catholic Standard* and the *Church of Ireland Gazette*, and for good measure a former Moderator of the Presbyterian Church gave a fifteen-minute BBC talk on the play. But McKee told me in forceful terms that if the play went on in full, the guns would be out, blood would flow and the theatre would be wrecked by mobs ... I felt it was the sort of talk that my son would have enjoyed ... he's a Lone Ranger fan." (Sam Thompson Collection).

Thompson accused McKee of assuming the role of Lord Chamberlain for Northern Ireland and asked that the public judge the play for themselves, as they were not 'thugs', as McKee had insisted, but rather decent and intelligent fellow-citizens. The controversy appeared in newspapers and gave major publicity for Thompson and his call for freedom in the arts. The board of directors issued a statement in which they addressed the controversial nature of the play and, in many respects, highlighted the plight of drama in Northern Ireland during the previous decades. In the board's view, it was necessary to stay away from issues that confronted an already worsening political and religious situation. It was the policy of the directors of the Ulster Group Theatre to keep religious and political controversies off the stage, as they feared a political play in the theatre would sooner or later spill onto the streets of Belfast. Under the Northern Ireland government, during the previous four decades, political, religious and social injustice flourished and those in power feared this exposure.

The Ulster Group Theatre split over the banning of the play and its founding member, Harold Goldblatt, with James Ellis and Maurice O'Callagan, resigned. The Group Theatre in 1940 was the amalgamation of three amateur companies that merged into a professional company under Harold Goldblatt. The company had given life and character to the theatre in Belfast in ways that theatregoers had not enjoyed before. Financial support had been problematic, as in every small theatre, but the problem was alleviated by the appointment of Ritchie McKee as chairman, as he had access to the public purse as Governor of the BBC in Belfast.

Many outstanding names from Ulster theatre emerge from the early years at the Group Theatre: Stephen Boyd, Colin Blakely, Margaret D'Arcy, Doreen Hepburn, Catherine Gibson, J.G. Devlin, James Ellis and many others who found careers in England and in the United States. James Ellis believed the Group should produce local writers with themes that might help boost audience attendance, such as Brian Friel's *Francophile* (1959), John Murphy's *The Country Boy* (1959) and Thompson's *Over the Bridge*.

Several days before rehearsals for *Over the Bridge* were to begin, Ritchie McKee asked for a copy of Thompson's script; Thompson refused. Eventually McKee obtained a copy that he duly passed around to the other directors who immediately demanded major revisions. A resolution to have the play withdrawn was carried by six votes to two. McKee was identified as the same person who had, some weeks earlier, as Northern Ireland's Governor of the BBC, been directed by the Prime Minister, Lord Brookeborough, to go to London to stop the second part of a television interview made in the United States with Siobhán McKenna who had referred to the IRA in favourable terms. In Thompson's reply to McKee's public statement for the withdrawal of the play he stated: "I wonder if Siobhanitis has anything to do with it?" (Devlin, 1985)

The board of directors believed *Over the Bridge* would offend the religious and political beliefs, or sensibilities, of the man (or woman) in the street, regardless of denomination or class in the community; it would give rise to sectarian or political controversy of an extreme nature. "This staggering repudiation of drama as a serious art form explains why the Council for the Encouragement of Music and the Arts, headed by McKee, was renamed by the indefatigable Thompson, the 'Council for the Encouragement of the Migration of Artists.'" (*Theatre Ireland*, 48. November-December 1985)

The controversy in Belfast piqued the interest of other theatre companies who wished to produce it elsewhere. Invitations to Dublin to meet with Louis Elliman and Stanley and Lee McCabe at the Olympia Theatre were put on hold, as Thompson was determined the people of Belfast should be the first to see his play. It was ironic that the controversy over the play would eventually lead to its first production at the Belfast Empire, which was a much larger theatre than the Group, and where it would play to full houses for a six-week run with over 40,000 people eventually seeing it during its runs in Belfast and Dublin. Thompson later sued the board of the Group for breach of contract and won.

James Ellis produced the play under the name Ulster Bridge Productions and managed to secure contracts for several of Ulster's leading actors. Rehearsals began late in 1959 with the opening night at the Belfast Empire Theatre on 26 January, 1960.

Thompson later recalled the night and its sense of foreboding as many thought there would be riots in and outside the theatre, necessitating a large police presence. But despite the nervous tensions, Thompson knew that the audience would not riot. Truth, according to Thompson, is unassailable because no matter how bitterly it is attacked it will prevail. There was silence when the final curtain went down before the audience went wild with applause as truth conquered in the theatre.

In Dublin the play was scheduled for a two-week run but extended to four weeks and would have continued if other cities had not been booked. Meeting Lord Killanin after the opening night in Dublin, Thompson recalled the generous offer of his home in Galway where he might find solitude and peace to work on his next play. It was here that Thompson completed his second major play *The Evangelist* (1963).

Stewart Parker met Thompson only briefly, in Dublin, but has said that he felt he knew the playwright very well. Parker was in his first year of undergraduate study at Queen's University, Belfast, when the *Over the Bridge* controversy rumbled across the city. In preparation for his 2,500 word introduction to the first published edition of *Over the Bridge* (1970), Parker met with Thompson's family, friends and the people he worked with in Belfast where he collected stories and anecdotes about his life and work. Thompson's character epitomised all that was best in the Belfast working-class Protestant as he was the 'other side of the coin' from the extremist and one of the country's most important dramatists.

The Evangelist (1963) was first performed at the Grand Opera House, Belfast and directed by Hilton Edwards. *Cemented With Love*, first shown on BBC television in 1965, was directed by Peter Luke and was later adapted for the stage by Tómas Mac Anna as part of the Dublin Theatre Festival in 1965. A fourth play, *The Masquerade*, might be regarded technically speaking as a finished play as there are no apparent gaps or scenes missing, but there are minor errors and unevenness with an overall lack of consistency.

Sam Thompson changed the face of Ulster Theatre and his influence was paramount for Parker in seeking a way to move forward from the abyss of the past towards a more tolerant society. In his comment to James Ellis in the Elbow Rooms, a Belfast actors' pub, that he had written a play that no one would touch, Thompson was clearly aware of the controversial subject matter of his work. The rejection of this work by the Group's board of directors, was, as Parker had stated, "the most astounding repudiation of the theatre as a serious art form that he had ever heard. For while the maintaining of quiescence in the face of injustice is clearly in the interest of estate agents, it is by no means evident that it is the duty of the arts and if a dramatist could place no serious issue for an audience to consider, then what was the theatre for?" (Keyes, 12)

Thompson was not just a promising playwright, but one from whom might confidently be expected more and greater works. The fact that *Over the Bridge* achieved such notoriety had more negative than positive consequences for Thompson. It cast a shadow over the remainder of his work and made an unbiased assessment difficult, if not impossible. His premature death in February 1965 left little time to right the one-sided impression that had been created of his work by the press and the media generally, however, a new era in Ulster playwriting was foretold in his work and Edwards-Mac Liammoir Productions in Dublin were congratulated for bringing this renaissance of Northern writing to the attention of the Southern public in the Hilton Edwards production of *The Evangelist* in 1963. The Dublin Theatre Festival would have similar foresight in producing Parker's *Spokesong* in 1974. Thompson's death left a void in Ulster playwriting for some years. His legacy of Ulster plays informed the work of Stewart Parker and Gary Mitchell and the work of several women playwrights in the 1980s and 1990s, particularly the work of Charabanc and its first production, *Lay Up Your Ends*.

Those who had not seen his work and considered him to be

one of 'themselves' mourned Thompson as a friend. Protestants in Northern Ireland are often portrayed as Unionists, Loyalists, fundamentalist Christians or members of the Orange Order. Thompson, Stewart Parker, Gary Mitchell and Marie Jones have stripped away the stereotype of the Northern Protestant and the complex struggles of sectarianism, public and private realities, allegiance and questions of identity. There has been a whole industry in Northern Ireland aimed at introducing the Catholic and Protestant traditions to each other. It has tried to reveal something much richer and much more interesting in a people with a multifaceted culture that varies according to religious background but also geography, class, gender and the choices made by thinking individuals. The imaginative territory of Sam Thompson pointed a way forward for other playwrights in the belief that theatre plays a pivotal role in a society in which a whole and complete culture has to be achieved.

The deep sense of cultural and political embarrassment experienced by Parker as a member of the 'lost tribe' was eventually one that he came to recognise as a source of riches and not the drawback he had imagined. Mitchell has also come to view his own background as a source of riches despite the misrepresentation of the Protestant culture. It is difficult for many in the Nationalist community to appreciate the passion with which Ulster Protestants, of whatever persuasion, view their position, and many nationalists also find it difficult to conceive of the existence or validity of an Ulster Protestant tradition.

Thompson had little contact with other dramatists of his time but he mastered his craft better than most in the Ulster tradition. His use of satire revealed that he was conscious of the Ulster tradition and marks him alongside other Irish satirists including Denis Johnston, Sean O'Casey and Gerald MacNamara. Parker, also a keen satirist, has stated that he was "shattered" after seeing the first production of *Over the Bridge*. Parker began to push the boundaries of the Ulster playwright, but unlike

Thompson, his introduction to the theatre was more informed through studies at Queen's University, where he was exposed to contemporary British dramatists: John Osborne, Harold Pinter, Tom Stoppard, and the new Americans playwrights: Sam Shepard and Edward Albee who played a major role in his development. Thompson had tried to improve the conditions for the working class in Northern Ireland by highlighting many social injustices in his plays. Parker, through his early experiments in the theatre, approached the subject matter more obliquely.

Parker mastered his craft, but always acknowledged that even though his work may not have evoked the raw emotions in Thompson's output, he was also writing about the complexities of life in Northern Ireland in a long series of plays that attempted to address the same issues but with very different theatrical means. Thompson's rather grim naturalism is replaced in Parker's work by a playful meta-dramatic style that is clearly reflected in *Three Plays for Ireland* that use fantasy and comedy to explore topics that Thompson addressed with angry, deliberately provocative realism.

CHAPTER THREE

Stewart Parker
Theories and Early Experiments

As he looked for the right mirror in which to reflect a troubled homeland, Stewart Parker's background, as with most Northern Irish playwrights, frequently surfaced in his plays. It has become a cliché in Northern Ireland to say that the Protestants of Ulster have had few dramatic voices to interpret the virtues of their tradition and, in so doing, to give them some new sense of their own identity.

Parker wrote from the inside of the Protestant heart and mind and from this position he could afford a black and scabrous humour about his own tribe. It would, of course, be absurd to categorise Parker as a Protestant writer, as if to confine him to the spiritual ghetto. Plays like the wryly-tender *Spokesong* drew on his Belfast roots, but stretches out to reach huge audiences in theatre and television. In *Northern Star*, his play about Henry Joy McCracken, which exposed the mystique of Northern Republicanism, and in the eloquent and powerful *Pentecost*, Parker examined the Ulster Protestant tradition in a way which nobody outside that community could have attempted. The plays also presented a challenge for the Nationalists in his audience as they re-examined the lives and prejudices of Protestants.

Never easy on either his audience or his culture Parker is often referred to as the Irish Tom Stoppard. He was, without doubt, the most consistently experimental contemporary Irish playwright: "Calling realism a spectrum and naturalism the dominant theatrical convention of the present age, Parker instead focuses on playwrights who deliberately violate the first premise of the convention—that the audience should be as convinced as possible that what it is witnessing is actuality, not artifice. As if mapping a strategy for his own later work, Parker professed interest in playwrights who not only do not conceal artifice but also use techniques that make artifice part of the play's whole meaning." (Harris, 290).

Parker's writing was informed by an Irish sensibility, mixing humour, tragedy and absurdity. He lived through one of the most violent periods in Irish history and as a dramatist he sought ways of breaking free of the past to point a way forward with new forms of inclusiveness in which drama could be re-invented to transform narrow perspectives on history. This meant re-thinking theatre in ways that no other dramatist from the North of Ireland had attempted; Parker directed his writing to what theatre could be and should do. He was indebted to the work of Yeats, Joyce and Beckett in attempting to establish a dramatic context for theatre in Northern Ireland that is inclusive and visionary.

The challenge of forging a unifying dramatic image for Northern Ireland was central to all of Parker's work. The tribal, sectarian malevolence in the society is, according to Parker, the deepest and most enduring and least tractable evil in northern Irish inheritance: "It is not the border or the discrimination, not the corruption nor any other of the repellent symptoms ... I see no point in writing a 'plea' for unity between Prods and Taigs. What use has that piety been? I can only see a point in actually embodying that unity, practicing that inclusiveness, in an artistic image; creating it as an act of the imagination, postulating it before an audience." (Parker 8, 1986)

Parker (1941-1988) was born into what he described as "an average unionist family" in Ballyhackamore, in Protestant east Belfast, where he inherited the staunch and realistic disposition of an east Belfast ancestry. Many of the most maverick Irish playwrights lived in exile and its famous genius for exile has often been considered the nation's most authentic artistic gift. However, despite the distance travelled, the Irish writer never seemed that far from home. When he left Belfast feeling that he would never return, Parker commented that he was born, reared, and scarred in the city and was never able to leave it totally behind him.

Parker's birthplace was, like that of Sam Thompson, the key to all his work and was much more than just background or influence. It inspired and provoked almost everything he wrote. At Ashfield School in east Belfast, John Malone introduced him to acting and encouraged him to bewilder his classmates with his Christmas gift of a homemade magician kit. This was the first time, as Parker later recalled, that he was able to 'put one over' on an audience and also the experience which inspired his play *Nightshade* (1980).

In the 1955 programme of the school play, *Everyman*, directed and produced by John Malone, he appeared as Everyman. He was thirteen at the time but remembered the feel of the experience with an undimmed intensity since it constituted his introduction to the theatre that would become his life's work. John Malone was an enthusiast who responded with warmth and delight to the enthusiasm of others and in particular to those of his pupils: "In his openness and sensitivity to my own, blind, gawky, fledgling creative impulses, he succeeded in teaching me at that early age that there is a necessary vital polarity in drama between Everyman and the sleight of hand, between the Four Last Things and the three card trick, between poetry and patter, art and show business. It was the first and greatest of all the many debts to him which I incurred over the years." (Parker 5, 1986)

Everyman had a profound influence on him for the rest of his life as he believed there was a powerful force at work in the play: "We can, of course, acknowledge with our heads the underlying meaning of the allegory that our knowledge will point us toward salvation if we can allow ourselves to be guided by it. But all this is bypassed by our far more profound emotional response as an audience to a gesture of charity and a solidarity that transforms the whole human journey for us at last with a possibility of hope. It is a particular and yet a universal moment which we encounter in many other places." (Parker 5, 1986)

As a teenage poet, Parker was writing about how desperately unfair life had been and what a lonely soul he had been with unrequited love, passionate focus and desperate infatuations. While he continued to write poetry he was also slowly working himself to the point where he could write for the theatre. He discovered that he could incorporate the poetic impulse into a dramatic framework. Writing a play was for him a more sophisticated exercise than poetry; because it was a collaborative medium it involved thinking into the minds of disparate characters and finding a language for them to reveal their characters and to tell their stories.

After fledgling years in drama with John Malone, Parker flourished at Sullivan Upper School and at Queen's University. Many literary leviathans emerged out of Belfast in the 1960s, including Seamus Heaney, Seamus Deane, Michael Longley, Derek Mahon, and James Simmons. The student community seems, in retrospect, to have been a creative ferment of talented young people supporting each other in their attempts at poetry and fiction as they experimented with writing and staging their own plays. Parker was amused when literary scholars referred to his class at Queen's as seminal, as he later stated that he, and his friends, always believed that if anything was happening it was in Dublin, London or New York and were craven in their deference as to what was going on elsewhere.

As far as London was concerned, Parker felt as though he could as well have been living in Reykjavik as in Belfast, as all of the cultural influence was British. For Northern Irish Protestants there had always been a sense of ambivalence toward the two cultures. Northern Irish Catholics had a stronger sense of identity because they were unequivocally Irish whatever their passports or driving licences might say. Many of Parker's contemporaries either went to Dublin, Canada or Australia and pretended to be English there. During his undergraduate years he went through what he referred to as his 'Republican Phase' that was very common among young Northern Irish Protestants who attended colleges of higher education. The repression of Irish culture began during the formative primary and high school years when all culture was British; this emphasis created an Imperialist view of the world in which Northern Ireland was a colony. Those living in Northern Ireland had, since the partition of Ireland, always experienced their 'inferior' status as British subjects.

During the 1960s, Parker was known as an avant-garde writer, beginning his first publication in the Belfast Festival Poets series *The Casualty Meditates upon His Journey*. Seamus Heaney recalls with "particular affection and a pang of vicarious delight when Stewart rose to read his poems at the first meeting of Philip Hobsbaum's poetry group. The artificial aluminum leg he had worn since his second year at Queen's, when he had been stricken with bone cancer and undergone amputation encumbered him then. In spite of this, he lurched formally and significantly to his feet, a move which in retrospect gains great symbolic power. It was a signal of personal victory, of the triumph over demeaning circumstances, of the possibility of genial spirits in the face of destructive events. As such it had a meaning not only for himself but for the imaginative and spiritual life of Northern Ireland as a whole over the two decades that were to come." (Seamus Heaney, 1988)

Parker completed both his BA in English and an MA in poetic drama for which Philip Hobsbaum supervised his thesis: 'The Modern Poet as Dramatist: Some Aspects of Non-Realistic

Drama, with Special Reference to Eliot, Yeats, and cummings'. While reading Yeats at Queen's, Parker felt that he should learn to speak Irish and absorb himself in Irish culture but later he came to recognise that his background as a Northern Protestant could be a source of riches and not the drawback that he had imagined. Having the whole 'mish-mash' to draw on had great advantages in that it was possible to look at both British and Irish cultures from a slight distance. The contradiction of living in Ireland and looking longingly towards London as the capital is both funny and absurd.

After graduating from Queen's University, Parker went to the United States to teach at Hamilton College in Utica, New York. He lectured from 1964 to 1967 and from 1967 to 1969 he taught literature and writing at Cornell University. He returned to Belfast from the United States in August 1969 but went back to Cornell for several summer sessions until 1974, after which he pursued a full-time writing career in Belfast before moving to Edinburgh and in 1982 to London.

The 1960s were a good time to be young in America, as the student revolt had begun coupled with a widespread belief that individual principle and human warmth could prevail over institutionalised corruption and an oppressive state. Parker's peers were surprised when he moved to the United States. Seamus Heaney commented: "It was a move which left the rest of us who had known him at Queen's University feeling a little marginalised. Who would have thought that Stewart of all people, a natural domestic energy, would have upped and gone? He was indelibly the Ulsterman, low-key, astute, wry, merry, formidably and courageously himself: he seemed to belong to the verities of the home ground, yet suddenly he wasn't there. And the next thing he was back, talking familiarly about Archie, the American poet A.R. Ammons who taught at Hamilton, but who now sounded in Stewart's resolutely uncontaminated Belfast accent as if he were a foreman in Harland & Wolff's." (Seamus Heaney, 1988)

It was tempting for Parker to stay in the United States as the news reached him that violence was erupting on the streets in Northern Ireland. He believed that in order to write he needed to steer a course away from academia and literary criticism and to achieve this he needed to come back to Northern Ireland. He rejected the tradition of the émigré Irish writer exorcising his feelings about his birthplace in a mixture of sentimental recall and spiteful revenge for real or imagined persecution.

The return to Belfast coincided with the outbreak of the Troubles that continued unabated for over thirty years. Despite the fact that he did not live for much of the rest of his life in Belfast, the renewed contact released the subject matter in him: "Works of worldly humour that are so like an encounter over a malt whiskey with the man himself such as the collector's item book of *Bus Stories* and the radio play with the greatest of all titles *The Kamikaze Ground Staff Reunion Dinner* (1981) and the television play *Radio Pictures* (1985). A classic Parker scene emerges in his 1982 television play about his hero James Joyce in *Joyce in June* when Blazes Boylan gets his nickname by running across the operatic stage with his shoes on fire. Parker's glee at such things in real life was immense, as when in Louisville, Kentucky, he saw a St. Patrick's Day parade full of African-American children dressed in green and in a bar discovered green-dyed beer." (Dewhurst, 1988)

From Northern Ireland, he moved to Edinburgh and later to London, which became his permanent home. Frequent visits to the United States during the summer months were often accompanied by teaching courses in Joyce and assisting with summer productions. In 1969 he was in Ithaca assisting in the production of *The Hostage*, helping the actors with dialects and the politics behind the play. In 1974 he was involved, again at Ithaca, in a production of his own work, the radio play, *The Iceberg*. During this period he was also writing rock music criticism for the *Irish Times* and wondering if the academic life in the United States would have been less fraught than the one he had chosen.

Parker learned the craft of writing by producing several scripts for the BBC but his most creative work at this time was in journalism and particularly in his 'High Pop' music column for the *Irish Times* which ran from 1970 to late 1976. He frequently punctuated his pieces with puns and word plays in a witty, perceptive, entertaining and informative manner that was rarely dull and nearly always original. These columns are an amazing insight into his work both in his vocabulary and his attitude to life. In describing a book on *The Story of the Blues* he wrote: "As a present, it's a gift. It costs seventy-five pence. Don't give it to anyone who has no interest in either music or history or sociology or poetry or human nature. Give them instead *Engelbert Humperdinck: The Authorised Biography*, by Don Short." (*Ibid*) Parker took all the writing commissions he could find, which were mostly arts reviews but there were also publicity handouts for the Pig Marketing Board that offered him untrammelled possibilities of pun and innuendo.

James Joyce was a major influence on Parker's writing and in his essay 'Me and Jim' he takes great delight in aligning himself next to Yeats and Joyce: "Their chthonic majesties, harmless parlour game might be to divide the pair of them, Yeatsians and Joyceans, the apostolic and the apostatic successions. It could maybe work, after a fashion, if less attention were paid to literary criteria than to the hazier questions of temperament, the sense of kinship, the frame of mind, the stance adopted towards native sod. My own mind was framed by an urban neighbourhood, a working-class family struggle towards petit-bourgeois values, recoil from home and church and country, and appetite for exile. Scarcely surprisingly I should declare for Jim." (Parker 32-34, 1982)

Upon his return from the United States Parker turned again to James Joyce's work. Stephen's theory of the aesthetic in *A Portrait of the Artist as a Young Man* designates drama as the highest of literary forms. As Parker stated: "I was conceived shortly after Joyce died, and grew up in a Protestant Unionist family in east Belfast and am chiefly employed in the writing of plays for stage, screen and radio. You might well ask, on any of these counts, what business I have affecting such a familiar tone towards James Augustine Joyce. The very fact of being at so many removes is a help, no doubt: a Dublin novelist of the forties, say, might conceivably have felt a trifle less insouciant, unless of course he happened to be Brian Nolan. But on the other hand, no writer in Ireland, of whatever hue or cry, can think of Joyce as less than contemporary. Most of what is currently being written, by comparison with the work of his greatness, seems hopelessly dated. His values with regard to sex, art, nationalism, religion and much else of substance continue to be well in advance of most of the populace." (*Ibid*)

The period during the early seventies of freelance writing included the plays for radio, volunteer teacher and creative writing classes at the Maze prison alongside the 'High Pop' column, all of which focused eventually towards his central ambition which was to write for the theatre. The first manifestation of this urgent demand was in *Spokesong*, his first serious play for the theatre, which received its world premiere at the Dublin Theatre Festival in 1975.

Parker had become a professional playwright despite the indifference to his work from the cultural establishment in Northern Ireland, an experience he shared with Sam Thompson, but for different reasons. He had tried and failed several times to have *Spokesong* performed in Belfast and later in Edinburgh, and this frustration led him to comment that playwriting was an impossible pursuit because you could never achieve perfection and it was always dependent on money. No one could have anticipated the triumphant staging of *Spokesong* on Broadway in New York at the Circle in the Square Theatre in 1978.

In Belfast, any aspiring young writer tended to turn to the BBC, which had an active policy of encouraging young talent. Michael Heffernan, the Northern Ireland Drama Producer for the BBC, helped Parker hone his craft on the radio play with his first work *The Iceberg* (1974), written in collaboration with

Heffernan. The 1970s had been frustrating years for playwrights from Northern Ireland; a dramatic response to the political situation was necessary but the appalling and intractable subject matter could induce artistic paralysis if approached directly. They were frustrating times also in more practical ways; never had writers been more desperate to write and yet never had the indigenous theatre been less interested in staging their work.

Michael Heffernan, who encouraged the work of a new wave of Ulster playwrights, realised the power of the radio as a potential platform for reaching a very wide audience. Perhaps Heffernan and Parker got on so well because their lives were both blighted by potentially fatal conditions. Parker lost a leg to cancer in his early twenties and Michael Heffernan had to have repeated heart operations (from which he died in 1985). Both men shared a sense of mortality that showed in the tough, black humour of their work. (Cooper, 1989)

Drama constantly demands that it be reinvented. New forms of inclusiveness need to be discovered and shown to cater adequately for a contemporary audience. In this way Parker's expectations were that the theatre might create harmony through a shared experience that he felt was consistent with its ritual beginnings of mythic, death-and-rebirth themes. The theatre's effect on its audience is for the most part subtle and it was unlikely that theatre in Northern Ireland would put an end to the violence when both sides of the religious divide found it difficult to speak to each other. The theatre's effect is, however, also cumulative and unquantifiable.

Parker outlines his dramatic agenda in 'Dramatis Personae' (1986). A major tradition in the twentieth-century has involved committed socialist playwriting with a didactic intention and its greatest and most influential exponent was Bertolt Brecht. Brecht was in his mid-twenties when he became a convinced Marxist and developed his new theories for theatre. Alongside his *Lehrstücke* or 'learning plays' and for a time his agit-prop theatre when he wrote a series of didactic cantatas with the composers Kurt Weill and

Paul Hindemith during the late 1920s in Germany. It was this theatre that attracted Parker as it opened new possibilities to find his own form of Northern Irish drama. In several of his plays Parker would find and re-work along Brechtian lines events in Northern Ireland's recent and mythic history.

Brechtianism has prevailed worldwide during the past half century with innovation in theatre design, direction and architecture. In Parker's terms this has been possible "because the cinema had already taken over the narcotic dream-massage function which it is far better equipped to perform, leaving the theatre free to flaunt its own machinery of artifice. In contemporary theatre we accept that the spotlights may be in our full view, that the set will probably suggest a place and its significance, rather than merely attempting a convincing facsimile of reality, that the actors may appear in several disparate roles or perhaps comment on the action and that through these and a multitude of other ways, we will remain conscious of ourselves as an audience in a theatre at a certain remove from the presentation, scrutinising it analytically." (Parker 9, 1986)

Parker was attracted to the sense of *Spass* or 'fun' in Brecht's work. It was tautological, according to Parker, to say that those who enjoy the process of thought will find pleasure in ideas, but what about the others? Are they not to be allowed into the theatre? And even those who enjoy learning, might they not enjoy it more efficiently at a good evening class than amidst the paraphernalia of stage presentation? What is the special extra thing that the theatre experience can offer them? In a word 'fun', which Brecht says so frequently. It occurs in an essay written at the start of his career before the production of his first play *Baal* when he describes the indifference felt by young writers like himself towards the established theatre of the day. They can see at a glance that there is no possible way of getting any 'fun' out of this. This also occurs during the end of Brecht's career in 1953 when he is discussing the Berliner Ensemble production of

THE LOST TRIBE IN THE MIRROR

Coriolanus, which he believed should communicate the fun of dealing with a slice of illuminated history.

In 1948, Brecht was writing his most mature ideas on the theatre that he fully expounds in *Small Organum for the Theatre* (1948), a work that Parker believed many of Brecht's adherents had chosen to ignore. A play should exist as an object of instruction and is tantamount to telling the audience that I know what is good for you. According to Parker, this same mentality of dogmatic authoritarianism was also present in much of the English drama of the 1960s and 1970s that was devoid of anything resembling fun or education.

Brecht in his Stockholm lecture 'On Experimental Theatre' (1939) defines the current trends in European drama as those which entertain and instruct: "The theatre has not been successful in fusing these ideas together and in his lecture Brecht reveals his own self-critical spirit as he grapples with the principles of the theatre of alienation and what this has come to mean. How can the theatre be both instructing and entertaining? How can it be divorced from spiritual dope traffic and turned from a home of illusions to a home of experiences?" (Parker 10, 1986)

This 'home of experiences' is for Parker a part of the working model of wholeness that he believed had eluded the contemporary Irish dramatist because of its past-dominated habit of mind. The time had come to cease picking over the entrails of the past, and begin to hint at a vision of the future and to find a new mythology: "Parker wanted to re-orient us away from a controversial focus on origins and towards the horizon of new possibility, which is the domain of the dramatist. In doing so the theatre may be purified of 'redundant and harmful mystification' and rescued from the distorting strategies of reactionary domination and made into a genuine anticipation of freedom. Play for Stewart Parker can only happen when there is a creative relationship between the ideal and the real, between representations of pre-existing traditions and projected utopias. If the course of history is to be positively transformed, the

[60]

forward look must critically reappropriate and reinterpret the backward look, while at the same time guarding against the orthodox stereotypes of the past." (Andrews, 1989, April-June)

Parker finds himself on some common ground with Brecht as he shares Brecht's desire to change the world. He states that a play has an instructional capability and that we learn nothing of consequence other than through play. Brecht is exemplary in his concern to make learning pleasurable as he demonstrates how the didactic impulse can be subsumed within the ludic. This is a theatre, according to Brecht, that will be neither didactic nor absurdist and will aim to inspire rather than instruct, to offer ideas and attitudes in a spirit of critical enquiry as a challenge rather than a riddle and above all to assert the play-impulse over the death wish.

Parker could arrest play and enforce closure as he pointed to the versions of the historical myths sacred to each of the communities in Northern Ireland, not in the spirit of mockery, but in the spirit of realism and out of a desire to substitute vibrant and authentic myths for false and destructive ones on which the population had been raised. The challenge for Parker was to find a form that would accommodate the two functions of theatre that together would fulfil the wish for freedom and would include theatre as an open-ended process of transformation whereby pre-existing codes of perception and experience are deconstructed and theatre as a constructive and magical act can lead to alternative worlds: "This alternative world is the choice Parker wanted his Northern Irish countrymen to make and he modelled the reconciliation for them. Parker wanted to: torch, burn, turf, flay, scourge, expunge every old view, every old hurt, every old story, every old way of treating each other until they cry out in the darkness and embrace humanity until they can move from pastness to wholeness." (Harris 233-41, 1991)

The form of play in which Parker succeeded in making his fellow man 'cry out in the darkness' was also one that he shared with Samuel Beckett. Beckett dramatises the central ineradicable fact of play in human existence, and even in Beckett's bleak world there still exists the possibility of hope. If James Joyce had the different gifts of a mimic, a solo act with star billing, out in the big spotlight, Beckett was, according to Parker: "a man possessed by voices if ever there was one. The unique form of lyric-nightmare-comedy which Beckett perfected, has left its mark on the work of most playwrights who have started work since the premiere of *Waiting for Godot* ... In terms of a profane sainthood, Joyce was a missionary and Beckett a monk: the one storming around Europe acquiring disciples and enemies, the other solitary in the anchorite's cell of his own consciousness. You can talk back to Joyce." (Parker 33, 1982)

Beckett's characters survive their bleak existence, and just at the moment when all hope seems to be lost, he employs both the instinct to play while also inviting us to face the bleak truth of his vision. Play, according to Parker, is by its very nature the antithesis of nihilism and despair and is why he prefers 'Theatre of the Ludicrous' to 'Theatre of the Absurd' as a description of his own plays. In the theatre of Samuel Beckett the dignity of man is an illusion, as it is a struggle between the prospect of metaphysical nihilism and the refusal to be dumbfounded, despite the grim spiritual suffering that surrounds us.

With his humanist agenda and his faith in mind and man, Parker conflates a 'working model of wholeness' as he examines the state of Irish theatre and his vision of its future direction. He confirms that the legacy of the Abbey Theatre is spent, and that the writing of Sean O'Casey was moving towards two kinds of playwriting that are now conspicuous by their absence in Ireland, experimentalism and politically committed work. This work should have entered into the mainstream of an Irish repertoire which would have prevented Parker from assailing yet again the profound suspicion of ideas in Irish culture, its conservatism and its self-satisfied provincialism.

The total view of art envisioned for theatre in Germany,

Russia and Scandinavia was shared in literary Dublin. Yeats and Lady Gregory were concerned foremost with a literary theatre with the theatrical elements drawn mostly from an amateur movement. The Abbey was established as a writer's and actor's theatre of naturalistic comedy and not as a director's or philosopher-showman's theatre. This set the pattern for theatre in Ireland and one that Parker bemoaned, as there was no substantial body of theory except for Yeats' writing. Yeats, who understood the theatre thoroughly, realised that as a popular medium it could not be made to accomplish his ends and so accordingly he turned his back on it. When we use the words 'Irish Drama' we usually refer to the mainstream drama at the Abbey: Synge, O'Casey and Behan.

The international expectations from an Irish playwright could be categorised as follows: wit, extravagant language, shiftless but funny characters and pathos and hilarity intermingled. The cultural forces that underlie these qualities make them standard fare for the Irish dramatist as Broadway and London's West End continue to fill their theatres with kitchen-sink Irish drama. Parker's conclusion was that Irish playwrights have in common an unconscious impulse to express the most ancient element in playacting that is the instinct for play itself.

The instinct for play began in Parker's first major work for the theatre, *Spokesong*, that has its unifying image in a decrepit bicycle shop. *Spokesong*, despite its violent undertones, ambushes the audience pleasurably with the subject of the history of the bicycle and the invention by John Dunlop of the pneumatic tyre in Belfast: "Theatre is the most civilized and subtle of public games that we play, and the audience is a corporate player who has licensed the playwright and actors to counterfeit reality. The licit counterfeiting is consciously entered into by both parties and an alert and responsive audience which has chosen freely to play is essential to the game and is as essential as the high degree of craft and skill on the stage, otherwise the occasion would lapse into earnestness or attitudinising and the alchemy of pleasure and enlightenment would be lost." (Parker 11, 1981)

Parker was also indebted to Johan Huizinga's *Homo Ludens,* a work that informs the central thesis in his John Malone Memorial Lecture. Huizinga, he states, "affirms our subjectivity as the spring of all that is eccentric, fugitive, heroic or weak. Play is a process by which the given world may be imaginatively transformed, lack of playfulness signifies a kind of spiritual inertia, an imaginative death, a passive acceptance of normal reality. A man reduced to a system of external relations is a thing, not a man. Through his behaviour he flows out and into the world and it, in turn, permeates and conditions him." (Parker 16, 1986)

Huizinga believed the play spirit began to wane in the eighteenth century and has been all but extinguished by the conditions of modern life. The idea of a theatre that Parker found highly congenial is 'Ludic Theatre' celebrating and re-enacting the mystery of play and then performing a crucial function in society. Parker believed that theatre needed to confront the central issues of Western society and not only those of Crossmaglen and Connemara. The precedents set by Yeats and Joyce are invaluable as they have shown how to deal with Ireland as a manageable microcosm of the whole of Western culture. Parker was under no illusion that theatre foyers in Dublin, Cork, Derry and Belfast would suddenly fill up with budding Antonin Artauds, Jerzy Grotowoskis, Joseph Papps or Joan Littlewoods because of his work.

"From the point of view of the world, wholly determined by the operation of blind forces, play would be altogether superfluous. Play only becomes possible, thinkable and understandable when an influx of mind breaks down the absolute determinism of the cosmos. The very existence of Play continually confirms the supralogical nature of the human situation ... We play and we know that we play, so we must be more than merely rational beings, for play is irrational. In returning to the play-spirit Huizinga believed the mental sphere from which drama springs knows no distinction and seriousness and he reminds us that with Aeschylus the experience of the most formidable seriousness is accomplished in the form of play and with Euripides the tone wavers between profound seriousness and frivolity. The true poet, says Socrates in Plato's *Symposium*, must be tragic and comic at once and the whole of human life must be felt as a blend of tragedy and comedy." (Parker 10, 1986)

Play is therefore, according to Parker, "not wholly dependent on language or a function of it and subjectivity is not wholly constructed out of society's symbol systems as the act of Play asserts indeterminacy and individual freedom. Play, when it is freed from the connotations of 'frivolity and infantilism', which attach themselves to it in our work-ethic culture, is no mere diversion or idle escapism." (Andrews 1989, April/June) The pattern of play that is rooted in Parker's background and experience is revealed in his flexible and adventurous talent as it travels well from one medium to another. His success rests on that rare combination of popularity and integrity and an exciting experimentalism.

By 1979, Parker had been making his living from writing almost exclusively for the theatre and had lived in Belfast for almost ten years. He had already established his reputation on the international stage both in the West End of London and on Broadway. *Spokesong* demonstrated his success in showing how, in the face of a modern world with its distorted values through the commercial work ethic, life could be transformed and celebrated. "Parker's kind of play is spontaneously 'protestant', protestant in the root sense of the word, opposing itself to congealed meanings, refusing to be locked into the given cultural order of types. It is a semiotic force which interrogates and disrupts given identities, stable meanings and institutions, with a view to producing a new human subject, what Parker calls a working model of wholeness." (Dewhurst, 1988)

After the success of *The Iceberg*, Parker believed that his future

[65]

as a writer was in theatre: "I was thirty-three years old and I had fooled around for long enough, trying out and discarding a succession of roles: poet, academic, broadcaster, and rock music critic among others. Writing was my vocation. I was living through a war in my home town; there was no time to be lost. I had a vision of life urgently demanding an audience." (Dewhurst, 1988) Parker's passion was to write for the stage and most of all he wanted to experiment with theatrical style. Some exploration of Irish history and conflict was inevitable but he rejected the easy notion of putting on stage anguished and suffering citizens bemoaning their fate as he sought to engage and beguile rather than preach at a theatre audience.

Theatre is often viewed as threatening because it explores, in any particular culture, according to Richard Schechner, what is problematical, taboo, difficult, liminal and dangerous. The theatre could even become a rehearsal for a revolution as politics takes to the stage often in Ireland and more notably in the past thirty years in Northern Ireland where the theatre has confronted political issues more directly than any other medium. Theatre in Ireland is unique in a troubled world because it plays such a large part in its expression of self. Theatre in Ireland can also be of the most dangerous kind because it speaks a language that cannot be ignored and it is dangerous talk that people even pay to hear.

The question of what is worth dying for is a central theme in the work of several Northern Irish dramatists. Henry Joy McCracken in Parker's *Northern Star* (1984) goes to the gallows to save Ireland, while Peter O'Boyle saves his dignity in *Over the Bridge* knowing that he will die at the hands of the Protestant mob. This is echoed in Frank McGuinness' *Observe the Sons of Ulster Marching Towards the Somme* (1985) in which the characters Anderson and McIlwaine elaborate a parallel between the celebrations of the glorious Twelfth of July and their fighting at the front during the battle of the Somme during World War I. They translate Germans into Irish Catholics and the River

Somme into the River Boyne. The experience of the Somme is also linked to that of the Titanic, the pride of the Belfast shipyards whose fate induces a sense of doom and a collective disaster for the Protestant population of the north of Ireland.

In attempting to clarify what theatre could, and should, be in Northern Ireland, Stewart Parker was concerned with the theatre's ritual beginnings in mythic, death and rebirth themes. He admitted that being an Ulster playwright was a difficult and often dangerous occupation in saying what often goes unsaid on subjects that were taboo and emphasising what he considered to be vital theatre in 'Lilliput' or a country that could not even find a name for itself: "Writing about and from within this particular place and time is an enterprise full of traps and snares. The raw material of drama is over-abundant here, easy pickings. Domestic bickering, street wit, tension in the shadows, patrolling soldiers, a fight, an explosion, a shot, a tragic death: another Ulster play written. What statement has it made? That the situation is grim, that Catholics and Protestants hate each other, that it's all shocking and terribly sad, but that the human spirit is remarkably resilient for all that. Such a play certainly reflects aspects of life here. But it fails to reflect adequately upon them. To borrow ... from Brecht: If art reflects life it does so with special mirrors. Documentary journalism can reflect with accuracy real lives being lived. Art amplifies and distorts, seeking to alter perceptions to a purpose. A play which reflects complacent assumptions, which confirms lazy preconceptions, which fails to combine emotional honesty with coherent analysis, which goes in short for the easy answer, is in my view actually harmful. And yet, if ever a time and place cried out for the solace and rigour and passionate rejoinder of great drama, it is here and now. There is a whole culture to be achieved. The politicians, visionless almost to a man, are withdrawing into their sectarian stockades. It falls to the artists to construct a model of working wholeness by means of which the society can begin to hold up its head in the world." (Parker, 1986)

'Dramatis Personae' describes theatre that is the antithesis of martyrdom. The drama in Northern Ireland does not follow that of the well-made play and in most instances is in opposition to it. There is also the expectation that the Irish dramatist should write about the Troubles either directly or indirectly. The dramatist should function as a medium, according to Parker, and he should be half-hidden in darkness, subject to possession by ghosts of other voices, often truer than his own.

The experience of reading *Dubliners*, *A Portrait of the Artist*, *Ulysses* and Richard Ellmann's biography on James Joyce was a form of confirmation for Parker as there was so much that was familiar to him. In the tenacity of Joyce's emotional ties with Dublin, the possessive love, mingling with the obsessive execration, the struggle over the years to annex the place to the realm of his own imagination, Parker "saw mirrored, my own tangled involvement with Belfast. In his inexhaustible fascination with the idiosyncrasies of human character, I saw my own chief delight and preoccupation. In waging of art as a battle towards an ultimate affirmation of that character, I saw my own highest aspiration. And it warmed the cockles of my self-absorbed young heart." ('Me and Jim', 34)

Stewart Parker had strong family connections with the shipyard in Belfast and like most citizens of the city he had heard many of the stories told over the years about the history of the Titanic. *The Iceberg* (1974) is no ordinary retelling of the familiar Titanic story. The play was produced just six months after the workers' strike in Northern Ireland that precipitated the fall of the power sharing executive and the Sunningdale Agreement of 1974. Set on board the Titanic during its maiden and final voyage to America, *The Iceberg* is a witty and angry allegory of Ireland's political and social conditions and is a major play by any standard, marking the beginning of an impressive body of work which continued until Parker's untimely death in 1988. *The Iceberg* shows Parker's ability to debunk pretension and pomposity with humour in challenging the sacred self-defeating myths of history and his hatred of the ritual celebration of pain and division. Most importantly it reveals a terrible understanding of what might have been, in Parker's words, "if only we had got it right". The politics of the period are omnipresent throughout the play through references to the Irish Home Rule Bill of the early twentieth century.

The Iceberg is a radio play in which Parker constructs a dialogue between the ghosts of Danny and Hugh, two workers killed during the construction of the *Titanic* at the Harland & Wolff. Parker places the conscience of Belfast in the ghost workers as they view the legacy of the *Titanic*. Edna Longley in 'The Writer and Belfast' states that Belfast for many writers has been home and a major source of inspiration, but of course no city, whatever the condition of its literary culture, may presume to be called the Muses' home. The 'Muses' in the mid-nineteen seventies were not easy to find with a bloody civil war that provoked a dramatic response to the crisis. Radio was of great importance to young writers during this time as it was difficult to have work staged in the main theatres and it also allowed for unlimited imaginative scope in setting genre whilst appealing to a large audience across the country. Radio also provided an enormous potential for contemporary drama that was promoted by the BBC. *The Iceberg* was forged out of the violence in Northern Ireland and it gave Parker a large listening audience.

Many critics found Parker's dramatic method hard to understand, especially his choice to tie the critique of Belfast to the history of cycling in *Spokesong* and to the wreck of the *Titanic* in *The Iceberg*. Hugh and Danny are shipyard workers in overalls who are presented realistically and backed by a chorus of musicians all of whom appear in evening dress and white face. The setting is a stylised arrangement of rostra at different levels connected by steps and ladders and at the highest point a lifeboat davit with the stem of the lifeboat suspended from it: "This setting could suggest the kind of symbolic verse drama written by W.H. Auden and Christopher Isherwood in the portentous shadow of German Expressionism or perhaps Piscator's early *Volksbühne* productions. *The Iceberg* and Parker's later plays avoid the solemn philosophising, the stylised presentation of representative personages and enormous societal pressures and the general earnestness of Expressionism. They also avoid post-war realism and the intensity of Piscator's political theatre with its bold experimentalism, movie projections and use of propaganda. *The Iceberg* foreshadows much of Parker's later work and is nearer to the native British tradition of music hall." (Parkin, 136)

The use of metaphor was, for Parker, the perfect device in writing *The Iceberg*. His use of ghostly figures from the historical past points to the influence of W.B. Yeats, with particular reference to *The Shadowy Waters*, *Purgatory*, *The Dreaming of the Bones* and *The Only Jealousy of Emer*, all with similar supernatural figures. In *The Iceberg* the ghosts become modern workmen, and in his later plays, *Northern Star* and *Heavenly Bodies*, they become historical figures.

Hugh and Danny are closely aligned to the ghosts in Yeats' *Purgatory* who dwell in a ruined house, a dominant image of Ascendancy Ireland. Parker is indebted to Yeats in linking his characters to a central unifying image as well as in his use of chorus figures. The 'rhythm of metaphor', as Yeats referred to it, seemed to him the perfect device for setting the scene, creating the mood and fuelling the verse in his dance plays. Parker's use of the unifying image is tied to a very different dramatic and theatrical style. The white faces of the musicians in *The Iceberg*, for example, are given alienating anonymity so that they function clearly as a chorus.

The Iceberg is a witty, angry allegory of Ireland's political and social condition as two Harland & Wolff riveters find themselves destined to roam the decks of the ship. The riveters represent many workers who died during the building of the ocean liner, which they will now accompany on its maiden—and final—voyage. Hugh and Danny had died during the construction of the *Titanic* and now look back at their own funerals which they could see from the top of the shipyard gantries: "We were plunging down together. I lost my grip on your arm. The gantry and the water and the town were spinning round like wreckage ... I could see the sheer side of the boat, rushing right past me." (13) The Bandmaster, in the character of Thomas Andrews, the ship's architect, orders Hugh and Danny around the ship as the other musicians double as the Tour Guide and the passengers.

The simplicity of the plot is complicated not by action so much as by language itself, especially in its figurative effects. The ship is a theatrical symbol of human hubris, specifically in the form of the doomed British Empire. Parker evokes the greatness and wealth of the British past in the Tour Guide's descriptions of the ship's interior with fittings and décor in the style of William and Mary. This symbolism carries its own ironies within the overall irony of the ship's fate revealed in the detail of the ornamental clock with the female figures holding a crown above it to represent 'Honour and Glory' crowning time. The light humour of the Guide with a flock of tourists is inextricably linked with the bitter taste of lost hopes as the ensuing disaster is kept well in the background but close enough to shadow the comic foreground. This comic irony becomes an abiding characteristic of Parker's style in his stage plays *Spokesong* and *Catchpenny Twist*.

Hugh and Danny act as our spiritual guides: "The White Star Line welcomes you aboard our newest Royal Mail Steamer, *Titanic*. We are standing in the grand entrance of the forward main staircase ... It is designed in the style of the time of William and Mary ... the dome of stained glass is designed to give light to the staircase and grandeur to the whole entrance." (3) The ship is undeniably a magnificent construction, as it seems to offer security, stability, order and every affectation and pretension of English land-based architecture. Everything on the ship is designed to make the passengers believe that they are in another safer place (such as a large English country house) but it is a ship of fools and an ancient image for the human condition. Parker continually undermines this illusion of a safe place as dark, violent underwater creaking and gushing punctuates the elegant sound picture as we visit areas of the ship where the cursing English stokers are carefully withheld from the sight of the first-class passengers. "Up on deck, is it? You haven't seen our lovely boiler room yet ... got some hairy red men in there, we have smelly big lads, real hot blood puddings" and they have also not seen the emigrants on the third-class decks and the dead cargo of those who helped build the ship.

Leaving Cork, the *Titanic*'s final port of call before the Atlantic crossing, Danny recites a well-known sentimental ballad by Thomas Moore: "Th'o the last glimpse of Erin with sorrow I see,/Yet wherever thou art shall Erin be to me,/In exile thy bosom shall still be my home,/And thine eyes make my climate wherever we roam." (37) Sentimentality, a reputed trait of the Irish, is one, which Hugh takes to task:

> HUGH: What a country ... look at it ... the wild soft green of it ... stuffed full of itself. Full of its corpses. All it leaves you with is a pain in your bones ...
>
> DANNY: Say what you like about the rest, but Ulster's number one in my book.
>
> HUGH: Ah, Ulster, Munster, what's the difference, they all whinge to the same tunes.
>
> DANNY: You don't need to tell me the difference. Look at that boat, can you imagine them building it in Cork or somewhere ... Belfast built, that means something, you know it does, Hughie. Workmanship—all over the world. It wasn't bogtrotters that built this ship. (37-38)

Belfast had to import all the raw material necessary for shipbuilding. The *Titanic* was built for "John Jacob Astor and his millionaire Yankee cronies" most of whom were unaware of where the ship was constructed, and knew nothing of the 'proud', poverty-stricken Belfast workers. The ship's southern

Irish doctor, in a conversation with Thomas Andrews, the *Titanic*'s northern architect, discusses the Act of Union and the racial stereotypes they represent. The dismal chain of Irish history, stretching from the *Titanic* disaster to the present, offers a sobering context in the minds of the audience as the friendly rivalry of the northerner Andrews and southerner O'Loughlin, reconcile at the end of the play: "Here's to your ship, Tommy. I'm proud to be your countryman, even if you disown me. Here's to your dream."

> O'LOUGHLIN: Thomas, I never love you more than when you are earnestly assuring me of your rationalism and you sitting there with your eyes full of stars. Sitting in the biggest ship in the world, which you built—in a country without the single raw material for the purpose—on a patch of reclaimed mud. No, we're far too sensible and workaday in the south—for the New Ireland to be complete, we'll need impractical wild dreamers like yourself and all those other mad Northerners. (54)

Danny's quip, "Did you read the one about the Boat Race? Both their boats got swamped, they both sunk. There was nobody left to be the winner" (7) is a metaphor of doomed Empire and the bitter rivalry between Protestants with Catholics in Northern Ireland. Danny's comment that he "has no desire to spend eternity living in a ship's lifeboat" is a reference to Ulster as a slice of Britain tenuously attached to the sinking ship of the Empire. The central metaphor is also extended in other ways through song, which is a recurring device throughout Parker's work. Dr. O'Loughlin plays the piano and sings a concert party number in which he praises Thomas Andrews' ship and its proof against the elements. The heavy irony is touched with poignancy from the waving gestures of the chorus as they move off in slow motion wearing fixed smiles on their faces suggesting vaudeville, rather than expressionism.

The doomed ship metaphor is developed further as Hugh suggests that newer and larger ships will be built in Belfast to compete in the race for even larger ocean liners. They will "put a slipway under Belfast and launch the whole cursed city into the river—after all the people have been shot by the army—for refusing to obey orders and abandon ship." Danny naively replies: "The Army'll never fire on loyal Ulstermen." (41-42) Thus, the metaphorical method has multiple layers of suggestion: the plight of the Ulstermen, seeing themselves as British, yet in danger of being legislated into union with the South, would be "abandoning" ship, yet the absurdity of a floating Belfast is also clear. The ambivalence and ambiguity of metaphor makes it the most likely verbal device, together with its cousin the pun, to capture the uncertainties, ambiguities and absurdities of the situation in Ireland.

The play ends with Hugh and Danny recalling their own deaths, and at this moment we hear the ship begin to break up although the sound is "nothing at all, the ship just shivered", at which point we hear underwater grinding and water flowing. As the ship breaks up it suggests the plight of the people of Ulster and that the treaty upon which Ulster was founded now founders on *The Iceberg* of terrorism. The light-hearted tone, the jokes and the fun that characterise Parker's style are set against the essentially pessimistic metaphor of the ship.

The success of *The Iceberg*, as a radio drama, encouraged Parker to produce a major work for the theatre to incorporate his love of music onto the stage in a play that contrasts gentle *spokesong*s against the bigotry and violence in Northern Ireland. In attempting to portray a Belfast that is softer than the view the rest of the world has of that city, Parker reveals that beneath the seemingly cold exterior of the city there is warmth, humour, and bitter ironies in the bicycle shop of Frank Stock in *Spokesong*.

Spokesong had its premiere at the Dublin Theatre Festival in 1975 and was Parker's first serious move into the professional theatre. The play was the last of thirteen plays presented at the festival and opened during the second week at the John Player Theatre on Dublin's South Circular Road. The omens were not propitious in spite of the play's billing: A World Theatre Production of a World Premiere. As Parker later recalled, there were twelve other plays in the festival and *Spokesong* was thirteenth in the batting order.

Parker had submitted his first play, *Deirdre Porter*, which was written eight years before *Spokesong*, to the Lyric Theatre in Belfast, then one of the only viable theatres for new work. No response had been forthcoming for two years when a production was suddenly announced, but after consultations with the playwright about design and casting, the project quietly disappeared. At twenty-five years old Parker had an early initiation into the working of professional theatre: "At the time I was astounded by all this ... I have, of course, long since grown used to the neurotic, self-enraptured shambles which characterises theatre regimes the world over. Theatre people subsist on a diet of crisis. If good work emerges in the midst of all of this, as it occasionally does, then the writer, however battered and bemused, somehow copes with it. The Lyric Theatre did not produce *Spokesong* and it remained on the shelf in Belfast." (Parker, 1985)

To present *Spokesong* in the 'right way', an independent production was necessary and the Edinburgh Festival Fringe presented the most appropriate alternative venue. Parker began by enlisting Michael Heffernan, as a trusted friend and colleague from the BBC in Belfast, after his production assistance with *The Iceberg* in 1974. Heffernan lobbied the Arts Council to support the production and continued to advise Parker on the structure of the play. He suggested that the second act should be rewritten and Parker obliged. The production subsidy from the Arts Council was fraught with problems, as the Arts Council of Northern Ireland could not subsidise a work if it did not have its premiere there. Parker agreed to the terms but decided that he would raise sufficient funds to take the play to Edinburgh after the Belfast premiere. Heffernan and Parker established their own corporate identity under the title Ixion Productions to produce

Spokesong and persuaded several well-known figures to support the company including the solicitor Brian Garrett, a theatre enthusiast who directed an appeal for funds endorsed by three Belfast luminaries: Mary Peters, the Olympic triathlon winner, Sandy Scott, a shipyard trade unionist, and the actor James Ellis. The appeal went to the City Council, the Dunlop Tyre Company and twenty other commercial institutions requesting programme sponsorship.

The nucleus of a company was already underway for the first production with Steven Rea, an actor Parker had known since Queen's University days in Belfast, to play Frank Stock. Allan McClelland was to play Francis Stock, and, as both actors had established careers in London, Parker believed that they would help greatly in the first production in Belfast. This production did not, however, materialise. Having been assured by the Arts Council in January 1975 that funding was forthcoming, they discovered in May that the Arts Council had received a smaller government subvention and Ixion Productions would, therefore, receive no funding. There was one positive offer of seventy-five pounds for the company from British Rail. Parker later recalled that as an ironist he felt very keenly the poetic aptness of this donor whose services he would later engage to take a one-way journey out of Northern Ireland.

The premiere of *Spokesong* was now consigned to the Dublin Theatre Festival. The venue was, according to Parker, probably unique in Ireland and possibly in the world, as it was a constituent part of the Player-Wills cigarette factory and was consequently permeated with the smell of tobacco whilst being entirely devoid of a liquor licence. The theatre also had a flat oblong floor facing a flat-end stage, and, as many of the entrances and exists in *Spokesong* had to be accomplished on bicycles, the omens were not good.

The Dublin critics were enthusiastic and later the London critics were enraptured by the production. The Royal Court Theatre in London immediately showed interest in the play and the National Theatre of Belgium bought it. It was first produced in London by the King's Head Theatre, opening in September 1976, and ran for six months before a brief transfer to the West End. In November the play was being performed at the Theatre National in Brussels, where Parker was amused to hear his characters Frank and Daisy 'chatting up' in French. In February the following year Peter Ustinov presented Parker with the *Evening Standard* Award for the Most Promising Playwright of the year. Over the following years *Spokesong* was performed all over the world in Denmark, Finland, Norway, Sweden, Holland, Australia, New Zealand, Canada and the United States.

The play received its United States premiere at the Long Wharf Theatre in New Haven in 1978 and the following year on Broadway's Circle in the Square where the *New York Times* critic called it "a most funny and piercingly intelligent play which successfully captured the situation in Northern Ireland as an artistic vision. Stewart Parker has made art out of history in a tradition that goes back through Tolstoy and Stendhal. *Spokesong* is about life and not about a situation, or what in Belfast they like to call the situation. Yet in the inspired whirl of Mr. Parker's play, part fantasy, part vaudeville, with songs and skits, and all anchored to a very serious vision, the situation works as part of a most human fabric." (Eder, 1978)

In an interview with the *New York Times*, Parker commented that he was not a didactic dramatist but that he was trying to isolate what was at the heart of the turbulence in Northern Ireland, which meant not writing a play about Protestants and Catholics fighting each other, or another play about a paramilitary organisation. Such a dramatic approach, he believed, would only deal with the surface of the conflict and not look underneath to get to the core of what matters in the way we view the past, how we perceive it, and how to set up a healthy relationship with it.

The characters in *Spokesong* have conflicting relationships with history and with their own past as they struggle with

[77]

romantic nostalgia that involves disgust and contempt. Contemporary Irish theatre needed to view the nature of violence in Northern Ireland in such a way that the audience would be taken completely by surprise and caught without its preconceptions. To do this, Parker wrote about the history of the bicycle believing that it was the most unlikely way to get to the subject of Northern Ireland through the folklore of Belfast, and the fact that the pneumatic tyre was invented there by John Dunlop in 1887.

It is through the conflict between the brothers Frank and Julian Stock that Parker explores the violent confrontations in Belfast. Frank is convinced that the bicycle is the answer to the modern city's congestion. Replacing the automobile with the bicycle in the centre of the city would certainly stop the many car bombs which were demolishing Belfast's city centre. Coupled with this pragmatic solution, the bicycle also supports Frank's nostalgic vision of the past and a lost age of innocence.

Haunted by the decency of his grandparents, Francis and Kitty Stock, Frank finds their personal legacy decaying along with his shop that is under threat of demolition from the town planners and also from the paramilitary bombing campaign. Frank is really a minister in the secular religion of bicycle repair and a zealot in the cause of salvation by pedal power, and Parker, using this embattled creed as a metaphor, is able to shift the play back and forth seamlessly through the eighty years of the bicycle shop by questioning even a healthy methodology like Frank's. Frank resolutely confronts a hostile world when his brother Julian returns from London and tries to steal his girlfriend Daisy, before attempting to sell the business to her loyalist father. In this world of deception and avarice Frank feels bereft of love and his livelihood in the bicycle business is sustained by the hatred of his old adversary the automobile, a weapon of war whose apotheosis is the car bomb:

FRANK: What it all comes down to—is personal mobility in an area of five square miles. At the moment there's just five square miles of anger and internal combustion. But suppose all the cars could be banished ... What would be left? Buses. Taxis. Feet ... Imagine a fleet of civic bikes ... gleaming with the city's coat of arms ... stacked on the corner of every street ... which anybody can ride anywhere, free of charge inside the city centre. The clean air. The people healthy. The time saved. The energy conserved. Earth would have nothing to show more fair. (26) ... A car is just a hard shell of aggression. No wonder they are using them as bombs. It's a logical development. A bicycle hides nothing and threatens nothing. It does what it does, its form is its function. An automobile is a weapon of war. (40)

Julian is a photojournalist who moved to London to become an anarchist, but returns to Belfast to destroy Frank's romantic notions in an already corrupt society. Frank's painful education into the realities of Belfast life is a central theme in the play. There are also conventional love stories between Frank and Daisy and the grandparents Francis and Kitty. Through these relationships Parker explores the conflict between Catholic and Protestant and Republican and Unionist.

The play opens with a short scene introducing Frank and the Trick Cyclist and ends with the Trick Cyclist cycling off to the tune of 'Daisy Bell' ushering Daisy into the bicycle shop to ask Frank if he repairs bicycles. The meeting of Frank and Daisy is a witty encounter as Daisy laments the rust on her old bicycle while Frank tells her that what it needs is "a look, a smile, a lingering caress. It's crying for a bit of love and attention, like the rest of us." (8) Daisy is surprised when Frank refers to her as a school teacher as he astutely discerns the chalk dust between her index finger and the thumb. Frank expounds absurdly on the impressions left by the bicycle tyre:

DAISY: So I have started to look like a School Teacher.
FRANK: A certain authority of manner.
DAISY: Elementary, no doubt.

FRANK: But yes ... Holmes was shaking his head. A bicycle, certainly, but not THE bicycle, said he. I am familiar with forty-two different impressions left by tyres. This, as you perceive, is a Dunlop, with a patch on the outer cover. Heidigger's were Palmer's; leaving longitudinal stripes ... It is of course possible that a cunning man might change the tyres of his bicycle in order to leave unfamiliar tracks. A criminal who is capable of such a thought is a man whom I should be proud to do business with. (9)

Frank substitutes the bicycle for Daisy after she has left the shop, as he holds up the saddle and apostrophises to it:

FRANK: Would that I had been where you had been, kid. With trembling fingers he removed the spring clip from her chain and unhooked the connecting link ... a sense of wonder mingled with the swelling drumbeat of his desire, his hands sweeping across the firm young spokes, up to their nipple heads, until the soft pliant tyres yielded to his touch and sent his senses spinning. (10)

The developing romance between Frank and Daisy is couched in terms of a detailed description of the history of the bicycle. Frank describes to Daisy the problems in repairing her bicycle with a full history of the evolution of the bicycle from 3500 BC in lower Mesopotamia to the French in 1791, and then to the first commercially produced model in the 1860s. The opening of the Stock's bicycle shop in 1895 was the year of Oscar Wilde's libel suit and Parker delights in establishing the relationship between Frank and Daisy as a history lesson of salient events through the development of the bicycle.

Daisy is a pragmatist and despite the romantic dreams that Frank attaches to his shop and the bicycle she forces him to view his position with perspective: "Nobody could make a go of this business. Good God, in a building scheduled for demolition. Bombs going off all round you. Selling a product that went out of fashion almost twenty years ago." (57) (It is ironic that Daisy should later buy the business from the shameless egotist Julian, who had inherited the lease). Despite her reservations about Frank's idealism, she recognises the humane interest, the vitality and integrity, which lie behind it. What she sees in Frank is a balance of mind that permits him to acknowledge the poison of the past, but she encourages him to identify a positive inheritance which is supportive and in which he can take pride. That past is embodied for him in the figure of James Boyd Dunlop who, in the midst of chaos, brought to completion 'a dream as old as mankind' with the invention of the pneumatic tyre.

Daisy is tempted by Julian's offer of a safe haven in London but rejects his flashy appeal for Frank's stubborn heroism as the play resolves itself on a sentimental note, 'on a bicycle built for two': "The social and historical forces which have been at work to squeeze the life out of Frank are finally displaced by the old-fashioned message of love and hope, deriving from the conjunction of an idealistic courageous man and a strong level headed woman. A problem play dissolves into a naive and charming answer play." (Andrews, 1989 July/September)

The music in *Spokesong* is Parker's way of going off at a tangent and jolting the audience into seeing the material from a different perspective. The songs are there to convey a sense of the period spanning eighty years. It is a vertical rather than a linear play, with a simple story, but complex characters centring on the counterpoint between the plight of Northern Ireland and the conflict of the two brothers in an incongruous unifying image of a decrepit bicycle shop. Parker has stated that one of his strategies was to try to write a play about violence that would "ambush the audience with pleasure" and there are few subjects more pleasurable than the history of the bicycle. Social history is in tandem with the political history of the Unionist and Nationalist ideological divide that is both uncanny and provocative. The period from Dunlop's 1887 invention of the pneumatic tyre in Belfast to the ecology movement and bicycle revival of the early 1970s encompasses the end of Parnellism and Randolph Churchill to the Home Rule Bills, the Great War,

Partition of Ireland and right up to Bloody Sunday and Bloody Friday in more recent times.

Pervading this structure like a nostalgic perfume is first the story of Frank and his adopted brother Julian who were brought up by their grandparents after their father and mother were killed in the Belfast Blitz. The play centres on the family's wild, whimsical and happy concern with the bicycle in its pleasure and its history. The grandfather Francis Stock, who had wooed and won the flamboyant Kitty Carberry, founded the Bicycle Shop. They had been Victorian idealists of wildly conflicting opinions; Kitty was a Maud Gonne style Nationalist, while Francis was an Empire Loyalist. Francis went off to fight for King and Country during the Great War leaving Kitty to manage the bicycle shop:

> KITTY: Francis, when I married you, this business was disintegrating. You were renting this shop from one of your Presbyterian Unionist tycoons. It has taken me a very long time to turn your accounts to profit and to buy this shop for ourselves. And you are now proposing—at the behest of their royal English whoremasters—to cycle off to Flanders and leave me to cope with this entire enterprise alone. (41)

The only real bond between Kitty and Francis was their love affair for the bicycle that represented a form of love for humanity in which Kitty sees the bicycle as not only the salvation of Ireland but also the salvation of women. The play's impact comes from the mixing of the most unlikely material with the subplot flashbacks to the turn of the century and Kitty Carberry's suffragette and feminist standpoint, coupled with her relationship to her loyalist husband Francis. They are childless because Kitty refuses to bring a child into the world until she is given the vote. Kitty is a new woman of the 1890s who believes in the vote and, like Shaw's Vivie Warren, owns a lady's bicycle, is educated, and has a head for business and orderly accounts:

KITTY: Let us salute our instrument of potential freedom—Ireland's freedom and Women's freedom! The day is not far off when the tyrant on horseback will vanish from the face of rural Ireland ... A woman who has tasted the intoxicating freedom of the bicycle will never again torment her body with corseting, or suffocate it with skirts. She will hold at last her destiny in her own two hands. (66-67)

Kitty is ruthless in her Nationalist sentiment—she could not bring herself to marry an anti-Parnellite—while Francis is, in her view, part of this movement, even though he categorically protests that he is not even a Nationalist and could not take a stand on Parnell. Kitty admonishes Francis that it is better for him to be a self-avowed Unionist than a Pharisaical patriot. Francis' stand on Parnell and his abhorrence of his behaviour, which he felt he paid dearly for, releases a torrent of Nationalist sentiment from Kitty:

KITTY: One day, Francis, Ireland will be a sovereign nation, and womanhood will be a sovereign estate. Not until that day will the ghosts of Parnell and Mrs. O'Shea be laid to rest. (21)

Parker's metaphor astutely links the fate of Ireland to technological change when the Trick Cyclist becomes Dr. Peacock, whose pride and sexual repression is linked to the new technology. The Victorian puritanical, moral outrage links the new technology with dangerous socialist ideas and disgraceful sexual liberation. By implication the repressive prejudices of modern Ireland could be swept away in the rapid growth of modern technologies. Yet Parker switches straight from Peacock to Daisy, who tells us that schoolchildren in modern Belfast learn how to booby-trap vehicles. The implication is that repression spawns violence and that a new technology may simply be used for more violence.

Julian later dismisses Kitty as "a spoiled daughter of the regiment slumming it in the quaint back-streets and in her

[83]

ridiculous lace-curtain nationalism" and in an acrimonious outburst likewise dismisses Francis, "a vain and obsequious little Ulster tradesman, a crank and a bore, going over and over the same dog-eared tales of his youth and his war experiences." (60) Julian is the freewheeling anarchist unfettered and unconstrained by the social and political situation into which he has returned. He is a foil for Frank's stubborn heroism as he is determined to destroy the remaining vestiges of the bicycle shop along with any hope that Frank might have found in Daisy.

On one level, the play is the story of two contrasted yet slightly disparate wooings: Francis' of the sweet and self-determined Kitty and eighty years later the eccentric Frank's of the pragmatic Daisy who has been disillusioned by her experiences as a teacher as she attempts to educate children who are scarred and reminded daily of violence and atrocities. For her, the 'layer of granite that runs through this country' is impenetrable:

> DAISY: I found out the truth about this country at last. It's all granite all the way through—a great flat thick slab of granite. Oh, there's a rich vein of humanity in it, no doubt. But it's not worth quarrying, Frank. It's too narrow and too damned shallow. (57)

There is an inexhaustible flow of pun and allusion running through the lines which renders the dialogue rich and expansive as the play shifts between the living present and the life and times of the grandparents. This includes the period of Frank's youth when his grandparents raised him after the death of his own parents. The structure of the play demands that it shift between time frames, their appropriate vocabulary and speech patterns, as a cyclist changes gear by moving the chain from one chain wheel to another.

Stage directions for *Spokesong* indicate that the set should consist only of bare essentials that should all be real, allowing for swift transitions between the three acting areas. The styles of acting are also mainly realistic but include the vaudeville style of the Trick Cyclist and the performance of musical numbers. Parker's transitions are achieved in a number of ways but, like those of Thornton Wilder in *Our Town* and Peter Nichols' work in British theatre, they are mainly achieved through his use of the Trick Cyclist and his gift for presenting sad and even grim situations in a comic context.

In Act 2, one of the main transitions is made by the use of make-up and costume as Kitty and Francis appear for the first time as the older grandparents. Kitty bitterly states that if Ireland had been united, the German bombs that killed Frank's parents would never have fallen. The transition back from this scene is Frank's comment upon it which is an overtly thematic statement uttered as if he ponders the significance of his past life, linking the gaiety of the scene in which he made love to Daisy's bicycle within the larger context of love, war and the bicycle. Time as a continuum of transitions becomes part of the rhythm of metaphor by means of the repetitions of the *Spokesong* itself:

Each cyclist's favourite folksong,
Song of the spokes, Spokesong,
Whisp'ring through the years,
Music that's good for the ears,
Song of the spokes, Spokesong,
Spinning along through the gears. (45)

The four central characters in the play are more important as individual personalities rather than social products, they are sympathetic characters that we are not asked to view as in detached, critical, Brechtian theatre. The lives of Francis, Kitty, Frank and Daisy are viewed through the Trick Cyclist who acts as the chorus as well as the commentator and the critic who becomes caught up in a multitude of characters singing the songs that embody the spirit of Belfast.

Like the Bandmaster in *The Iceberg* the Trick Cyclist is a Master of Ceremonies—a clown, singer, conjurer and a thirties cocktail performer, as well as the spirit and creative force of entertainment in the theatre. He is Parker's quick change artist and appears as six different characters: public official, clergyman, Kitty's father, Daisy's father, Sergeant Major and plain clothes policeman, all of whom propel the action along in rapid transitions. These and other transitions Parker achieves with music and song push the theatrical conceit forward by means of stage business such as the spinning of a cycle wheel, light changes, changes in style and language, the action of cycling on and off stage and tossing official papers into the air to launch the closing chorus of Act 1. The offstage explosion brings the troubles to the foreground in Act 2.

The play opens with the Trick Cyclist's World War One song, "Daisy, Daisy / give me your answer do / I'm half crazy / All for the want of you, / It won't be a stylish marriage, / I can't afford a carriage, / But you'll look sweet, Upon the seat / of a bicycle built for two." (9) The song is performed from a unicycle upon which the Trick Cyclist rides around the stage as he introduces the opening scene. It is a quasi-courtroom scene that introduces Frank Stock, who vituperates on the problems caused by the internal combustion engine and the problems it is causing in the inner city. Frank's character is established by rapid dialogue between himself and the Trick Cyclist.

FRANK: It is just like this—the internal combustion has gone too far.
TRICK CYCLIST: Could I have your full name, please?
FRANK: Francis John Boyd Dunlop Stock.
TRICK CYCLIST: Thank you.
FRANK: Imagine the city as a giant body ... That's what it really is. Diagnosis—not good. Circulation sluggish. Lungs badly congested. Severe constipation. So what does this plan propose as a cure? Great Scott—a heart transplant!
TRICK CYCLIST: Sorry to butt in again, Mr. Stock ... Just to say, if you could be as concise as possible, for the sake of the other objectors ...
FRANK: Every morning, down they come, roaring and tumbling

headlong—the commuters—the gaberdine swine. They get to the intersection at the bottom—and immediately turn into a snarling, writhing, ravelled-up knot of ulcerous vindictiveness. We shouldn't be promoting that. We ought to be outlawing it. The time has come to rediscover the faithful bicycle. (6-7)

As the public official, the Trick Cyclist vents his concern about the public inquiry into the redevelopment of the inner city. A binding image in the play connects the personal life of Frank Stock with that of the city and the bicycle. The tandem effect that the bicycle conceit accumulates in the play is like the spokes radiating from the personal hub of the play's wheel in Frank and Daisy, to its public rim as the Troubles in Northern Ireland. The Trick Cyclist's instant adoption of an official manner and the language of local government quickly and fluently achieves all transitions in the public inquiry scenes. "The public inquiry is an image for theatre as plays on public themes have always been public inquiries in which theatre investigates matters of concern through the stage lives of its personae." (Parkin, 145)

The Trick Cyclist appears in Act 2 as Daisy's father, Duncan Bell, the loyalist paramilitary and a figure of intimidation and fear. There is a sense of bleakness in the scene as both Frank and Daisy realise the horror and intimidation under which they are living as Bell demands extortion and protection money for which he promises there will be no intimidation over Frank's shop. Frank refuses:

FRANK: Sorry, Duncan, count me out.

TRICK CYCLIST: What's the matter; have you no belief in law and order?

FRANK: Not when you phrase it in the abstract like that, no.

TRICK CYCLIST: A car bomb blows up across the street, and he doesn't believe in law and order.

FRANK: One army and one police force, that's already more than enough.

TRICK CYCLIST: The army and the police? You must be joking. It's urban guerrilla warfare, friend, against the likes of you and me.

[87]

It's a job we've got to do ourselves. I am disappointed in you, Frankie. I thought that you had more community spirit. (50)

The scene in which Francis and Kitty leave the lease of the shop to Julian and the business to Frank, to try to do right to both, is also suggestive of the state of Northern Ireland where neither British nor Irish jurisdiction has worked. Daisy, who eventually buys the business, expresses Parker's wary appraisal of the situation in the final stage in his recycling of the arguments about the north of Ireland:

> DAISY: Don't ask how this hellhole will ever redeem itself. All I know is, it'll only ever be done by taking account of the way people really are—all the people—in all their depravity as well as their sweet reason. (49)

The play on words suggest that folksong is a spokesong, or a song that speaks for the people, or a spook song, and the song of the dead. Folk songs address universals and speak across generations and traditions that juxtapose time past and present. The rich thematic cross-references in the play, of ghosts in a ghost-ridden cycle shop, are framed by the tentative knocking at the door of brash seventies sensibility. The audience is continually reminded in *Spokesong* of the construction of the dramatic illusion.

What is common in Parker's work is his reluctance to retread familiar ground. Each play has at its core incisive observations on life and in *Catchpenny Twist* (1977) the serious theme is packaged in entertainment and surprise. While 'nursing' *Spokesong* through its London run, and the many other productions planned for the play, Parker was under increasing pressure to write another play, which would prove as successful as *Spokesong*. Dramatists who have survived in the theatre after the success of a first play feel particularly vulnerable as they try to consolidate their reputation after an initial success and wonder if it will ever happen again. For Parker, *Catchpenny Twist* saw the beginning of a prolific period of eleven years of plays for the stage, radio, and television and, in his last years, the development of a new interest in writing for the cinema.

Catchpenny Twist was first performed at the Peacock Theatre in Dublin under the direction of Patrick Laffan. In December 1977, a television adaptation was broadcast on the BBC 'Play For Today' and in October 1978 it premiered in the United States at the Hartford Stage Company directed by Irene Lewis. The United Kingdom premiere was in February 1980 at the King's Head Theatre in London, directed by Robert Gillespie.

The setting for *Catchpenny Twist* is Belfast, Dublin and London in 1977, where teams of songwriters commit the error of writing songs for both the Protestant and Republican paramilitary organisations. For this, they suffer the inevitable consequences of attempting to be apolitical in Northern Ireland. Parker's lyrics and Shaun Davey's music infuse the play with the era of the Belfast Band Scene which had begun during the 1950s and continued into the 1970s until the violence forced the closure of most music venues.

The play is, according to Parker, "a charade with music" but in this description he is selling himself short. As he focuses on two innocent songwriters permanently on the run, he forces his audience to look at the inescapable shadow that has been cast by the Troubles in Northern Ireland. During the closing years of the 1970s, violence was still ravaging the streets of Belfast and bringing mayhem to life throughout the country while artists, songwriters and actors had continued to work under the most difficult circumstances in theatres and concert halls. In setting *Catchpenny Twist* in 1977, Parker focuses on the plight of the performing community trying to make a living in desperate circumstances. The plot centres on the lives of the naive Roy Fletcher and Martyn Semple, who find themselves in the midst of a paramilitary struggle from which they must run.

It was believed that cultural diversity was paramount if a

peaceful solution could be found to alleviate the political crisis in Northern Ireland during the late 1970s, and one of the main questions for community relations was whether to assimilate Catholics and Protestants or to accommodate the differences between them. The number of violent deaths relating to the Troubles had declined in Northern Ireland for the first time since 1971 and these figures would continue to fall over the next twenty years.

During the 1970s, social and political policies were loosely based on the hope that Northern Ireland had a large untapped middle ground between unionism and nationalism and that this 'silent majority' needed to be given confidence to make itself heard. To this end the government combined reform and support for moderate voices including the mainstream churches and such reconciliation bodies as the Corrymeela Community that had facilitated contact between Catholics and Protestants. By the late 1970s and early 1980s, it was apparent that the sectarian violence and politics were as persistent as ever and no middle ground could be found, as both camps were as far apart as ever, one decade after the Troubles began. As Parker commented: "Grow up in Northern Ireland today, and your every step is dogged by whichever of the two camps you were born into. You can surrender to it, react against it, and run away from it ... you can't ignore it. The past is alive and well and killing people in Belfast." (Parker, 1977)

Every place has troubles of its own, as Parker has stated in his author's notes for the play, but in Northern Ireland the history of the Troubles can be traced back through centuries of troubled Anglo/Irish relations. As Parker wrote: "When Americans talk about the past they might mean Watergate or Chappaquiddick, or may mean Dallas in 1963; when the Irish say the past they're gesturing back at least three hundred years to Cromwell and King Billy, and often beyond. How we deal with the past is the question which is often raised in Northern Ireland and to the present the record has not been very encouraging." (*Ibid*)

Catchpenny Twist emulates one of the Hope-Crosby 'Road' movies in which the guileless heroes find themselves caught up in some alien revolution but the difference here is that the bullets are real. Parker admired American scriptwriters with their clipped and poetic dialogue and he believed a playwright he should be a truth-teller and a sceptic in a credulous world: "But there has to be also an element of the medium in his make-up when he becomes possessed by other voices both divine and diabolic and they must be given their say; voices generated by the energy emanating from an intense moment of conflict, in a time and place though the time and place is always here and now during performance." (Billington, 1977)

As a "truth-teller" Parker is more brutal in *Catchpenny Twist* than in *Spokesong*. There was a glimmer of hope in *Spokesong* with the possibility that a solution could be found to the seemingly intractable conflict: "my own trite view of the world is that nobody's troubles are unique. Like the tension between the way we live now and the way we once lived, our present, versus our past ... however immediate or distant. For all of us, the past lurks in the undergrowth, poised for ambush. How do you deal with it?" (Parker, 1977)

In *Catchpenny Twist*, Parker focuses on the lives of two musicians in Belfast. Business is flourishing, and life is governed by neon-lit shopping malls, muzak, TV commercials and junk food in a brave new world, more seductive than the old one and murderous in its own inviting way. The incident that provided the dramatic material for *Catchpenny Twist* was the murder of the Miami Showband on 31 July, 1975. The horror and disgust expressed by the entire population of Ireland after the savage murders of the showband by the Ulster Volunteer Force affected Parker profoundly. This showband lived a peripatetic life between the north and south of Ireland trying to get as much work as possible from the music venues that had managed to survive the six years of the Troubles. The UVF stopped the musicians on the road and ordered them to line up in a field and shot them. They died because of where they lived and not because of what they did for a living. The bloodshed derived a horrific response from the sense that ancient and modern Ireland had taken flesh from one to wreak a blind atavistic revenge on the other. Parker grappled with this spectre of hate in the theatre, as it was the only forum in which he felt he could.

Although the play had its initial impulse from the Miami Showband murders, Parker did not use that event or any other actual event in the script as he believed the play's comic tone would be distasteful to some, and yet he believed that he had found a way of writing about a situation which was desperate. Including nine songs, *Catchpenny Twist* is filled with the music of the period, some of it tasteless and trite. The play relentlessly parodies the kitsch of 'Country & Irish', a genre "full of lachrymose self-pity, very much in accord with the Irish sensibility. Everybody I know, of my own age or younger, identifies the landmarks in their lives by means of hit records. And everybody who came up with Lennon and McCartney sees a songwriting partnership as the choicest form of heroism. For other generations it might have been actors, gangsters, or socialites. In the sixties it was songwriters, and I'm working with characters formed in adolescence by the sixties." (Parker, 1977)

A choric Vocal Trio, doubling as secondary characters, functions in *Catchpenny Twist* in much the same way as the Trick Cyclist in *Spokesong* with linking scenes and songs interspersing dialogue and commenting on the action. The central binding image is the *Catchpenny Twist* of the title (the game of tossing coins) but the image is now more than the all-pervading conceit found in *Spokesong,* as it is instead an answer to the riddle posed by the play's action in a charade that enacts clues to the riddle. Like a metaphor that has one foot in an experience and the other in a different but analogous one, the basic situation of the play tries to keep one foot in real life while one steps into the realm of myth or allegory or even parable. Parker chose to call the play a 'charade' as it highlighted the absurdity of life in Belfast in the 1970s.

The opening scenes in Act 1 are full of references to the violence that surrounds school life in Northern Ireland. The Headmaster warns: "I don't want to be reading any of your names in the headlines during this summer, I have no wish to see the good name of the school being dragged through the courts of law yet again and especially not in connection with guns and explosives." (80) The schoolchildren are already out in the streets fighting a war while Monagh, their teacher, complains that she is still trying to teach them 'The Skye Boat Song'.

After teaching for the past seven years in a public school, Roy, Martyn and Monagh are ready to leave their teaching positions and move on, questioning their relevance to the violence on the streets of Belfast. The Headmaster in an end-of-term frolic discovers them, which is a strip tease, vocalised by Roy and Martyn in which Monagh is in her underclothes; the Headmaster immediately fires his three unruly staff.

Turning to writing ballads for a living, Roy and Martyn find, in Monagh, their chanteuse who can sing the instant ballads for the dead Republican heroes alongside the witty gags for the Protestant comedians. When they boast to Marie, a militant Republican, that they are simply providing harmless entertainment, she retorts: "Nothing that mediocre is ever harmless." (40) Parker underlines that under the surface jauntiness, nothing in Northern Ireland is ever apolitical. Roy the tunesmith may describe his country as a 'pestilential swamp' and Martyn, the lyricist, may be more interested in internal rhymes than defiant gestures, but wherever they go they take their ancestry with them. Roy and Martyn are appealing and funny, and with mordant skill Parker manages to treat fanatics and European song contests with the same brand of amused contempt.

The narrative also involves Marie Kyle, who was a former colleague and is now a Republican who has taken up arms. An English television reporter, Playfair, with whom Monagh is involved, is 'gunned down' in Belfast. The plot is complicated enough for a problem play, but is not a direct narrative concern as these events flicker in the background and come only, at times, to the foreground. D.E.S. Maxwell comments: "*Catchpenny Twist* is like a sketch for melodrama going on as a backdrop to second-rate cabaret acts; if the play is in any line, it is that of Auden/Isherwood borrowings from Brecht in the nineteen thirties. It shares the same problems, are the songs good enough to listen to and are they bad enough to be parodies; the ballad-mongering, the pop scene, the private and public anguish—how do they connect?" (Maxwell, 184)

They connect through Roy and Martyn who are unemployed and trying to make extra money by creating street ballads for the paramilitary which offers "thirty pounds a throw". Faced with the problem of writing songs that have popular appeal, the duo struggle to find lyrics:

MARTYN: What's another word for 'nation'?
ROY: Country.
MARTYN: No good.
ROY: Land.
MARTYN: Longer.
ROY: Mausoleum ...
MARTYN: Then sing me with me this ballad of the death of Sean McVeigh, He will not be forgotten ... Not for a day or two, anyway. (83)

Many of the names of fallen martyrs do not find easy rhymes, and Quigley proves a difficult name to master. But other heroes are more successful in rhyme; McVeigh seems to rhyme in Martyn's song: "A British soldier cursed at him/As his life-blood ebbed away/But Ireland's sons will not forget,/The name of Sean McVeigh" (89). In a country full of hatred, the easiest thing to do is to make an enemy, as Roy and Martyn discover. They live between two devils, both of which want the best tunes. By the time they reach the artistic heights of composing jingles for 'Brady's Fried Chickens', someone is already planning to send a warning in the form of two bullets.

What is most appealing about Parker's work is the ease with which he blends lunatic humour with a gritty sense of reality that was achieved in *Spokesong* and again in *Catchpenny Twist* where it becomes ribald and hilarious: "The characters in the play are quick-witted innocents who are taking a surrealistic stroll across a minefield, cracking jokes in the dark, but they are also real people with a real past in an all-too-real city, making a living and terrified of dying." (Peter, 1980). His characters are real because their lives stretch beyond and outside the play. Creative distancing was needed to portray the horrific events taking place in Northern Ireland, and Parker evolved a style of writing to adequately contain these events and respond in a manner that used imagery and metaphor.

Robert Cushman has argued that even though Parker writes with a smouldering joviality that is very attractive, the play is to an extent the victim of its own inevitability. The characters are: "so plainly foredoomed that what they do en route or even who they are seems immaterial. Their deaths cannot really be blamed on their being apolitical." (Cushman, 1980) Parker delights, with his composer Shaun Davey, in exposing the puerility of the modern jingle and the ubiquitous songs from the Eurovision Song Contest. Roy and Martyn see a way of making a living in this popular industry and they are fully aware of its appalling standards and the popular culture that surrounds it. The songs, in ballad style, are too bad to be parodied as is exemplified in the 'Zig Zag Song':

> Sing hello the Zig Zag song
> Sing bye-bye the Zig Zag song
> It's a song that all can sing
> Come along and let it ring. (154)

As a musician, Parker was interested in the popular song. Early influences were American—Eddie Cochrane, Buddy Holly and Gene Vincent. Parker also stated that music was the ultimate art form. In his discussions with Shaun Davey, he suggested the compositions in *Catchpenny Twist* should be well-crafted parodies that could use the Eurovision contest as exemplars.

The rapid, quick-fire lines of the opening scenes are linked by musical interludes sung by Monagh, who has moved to Dublin where she sings in a sleazy nightclub run by a gin drinking, steel-tongued Mrs. Barker. Roy and Martyn join Monagh in Dublin after receiving two letters, one containing an offer from an agency keen on hearing their jingles and the other containing two bullets. Following the threat of reprisals from Belfast, Dublin seems for the moment a safe haven where they can resume their relationship with Monagh. Dublin provides temporary shelter before they must run again, and like Crosby, Hope and Lamour, they are soon on the road again, first to London and then to the Eurovision Song Contest where their past will meet with them.

Success eludes Roy and Martyn, and along the way they shed Monagh as they are convinced by the record boss that she is too old to make it in the world of popular song, "too old, too ordinary, and two-pence a dozen". Roy and Martyn should work with "a couple of schoolgirls we've recently signed. Dynamite voices. Lovely little things too. I think one of them is going to be very big." (141) In promoting their own lives Roy and Martyn destroy a connected life, and in recognising that what they produce is a 'gunk' commodity they, from time to time, express a wish for something more than a 'catchpenny life'. The dream of material success prevents them from ever making the break to greater authenticity.

"Roy and Martyn seek a rational explanation for their lives as 'Double Dealers' as they simply see people enjoying songs which to them are harmless entertainment. The focus of Parker's attention is in Roy and Martyn's attempted separation of art and politics that are held apart only by an act of bad faith. As it was for Mother Courage, there is money to be made out of war." (Andrews 26, 1989. April/June) There were many unscrupulous merchants in Northern Ireland who made their fortunes during the Troubles as they supplied both sides of the paramilitary organisations with military equipment and other daily necessities. Marie asserts that Roy and Martyn cannot be apolitical within the Northern Irish context, as the conflict and its repercussions cannot be ignored. Marie has a narrow historical perspective and argues that the past is what is important in the armed struggle, while Roy calls for a view of the future in which the past needs to be forgotten. Parker's own views lie in the middle of the impasse between his characters:

> MARIE: Where have you been the last seven years? The country's been at war, you know. A lot of chums of mine are in prison. A lot of chums of mine have given their lives ... I know where I stand. On eight hundred years of history, eight hundred years of repression, exploitation and attempted genocide ...
> ROY: I live in the twentieth century, love.
> MARIE: This time we're going to put an end to that for all time. There's unfinished business in this country ...
> ROY: You know, the twentieth century—aeroplanes, spin dryers. Pinball machines.
> MARIE: ... and you're involved as much as any other Irishman, which is right up over your ears, whether you want to be or not.
> ROY: You can keep your history. You belong in it. They should build museums for you instead of prisons. The rest of us want shot of it. (132)

Roy and Martyn believe they can exist outside history in a kind of agnosticism that is taken to be the mark of modern progressive thinking. To think they can deny belonging to a cultural tradition, a past and a class, Marie points out, is naive and deceptive, no more than an illusion and another example of inauthentic ideology. The truth of what she says is borne out at the end of the play when Roy and Martyn's dream of innocence detonates along with the bomb exploding in their faces. The self perpetuating myths of the past and the clinging to these very myths by Marie blind her. She cannot see the perversion in her own misconceived ideologies and tribal bigotry. What is needed as Parker states, are: "The alternative versions of historical myths sacred to each of the communities which must be staged, not in a spirit of mockery but in a spirit of realism, and out of a desire to substitute vibrant and authentic myths for the false and destructive ones on which we have been weaned. Drama can do this and much more, it can contain the conflicts and contradictions, the cruelty and the killings, the implacable ghosts, the unending rancour, pettiness and meanness of spirit, the poverty of imagination and evasion of truth which unites our two communities in their compact of mutual sterility and impotence all in a single image. Within that same single frame, it can demonstrate and celebrate a language as wholesome and nutritious as a wheaten farl, a stony wit and devious humour, an experimental vivacity and wholesomeness, a true instinct for hospitality and generosity, which also and equally unite our two communities." (Andrews, 19. July/September 1989)

The instinct for meanness of spirit and lack of imagination is embodied in Marie as there is no exit from one ideology without entrance into another. Without constant vigilance, beliefs can harden into an uncritical dogmatism that conceals its own practices of legitimisation and forgets its mediating function. The play is not concerned with the development of each of the characters but their role in the larger historical context. A play is a useless tool for dissuading people from killing each other, as Parker states in his author's notes for *Catchpenny Twist*: "It is not much better at persuading them to love one another particularly as the writer's intentions are usually subverted by his characters along the way. What a play can do is send out intangibles into the glare of a public arena and make them ponderable. The value of such activity has to remain an act of faith and cannot actually damage people to tell them a story, especially if you can make them laugh as you go along." (Parker, 1977)

This act of faith in *Catchpenny Twist* becomes immediately tangible in the closing scene of the play when Roy and Martyn's past lives finally catch up with them in the most unlikely place. Roy and Martyn's deaths have little shock value as they wait in the airport lounge for their flight back to London where they open the four greetings telegrams they have been sent for their song, presented at the Eurovision Song Contest and a larger package that they open last. In the author's stage directions, Martyn rips the tape off the package: "Simultaneously—Blackout. Explosion. A noisy drum intro. The band strikes up. A red spot comes on, showing MONAGH on her feet, smiling brightly, with a hand mike. ROY and MARTYN'S seats are toppled over. In the red glow, we see them on their knees, hands and faces covered in blood, groping about blindly. Monagh begins to sing one of the 'gunk' ballads, 'Laugh and the world laughs with you, Cry and you cry alone.'" (159)

By intensifying his satiric thrust at this point and driving it into macabre realism, Parker emphasises corrective irony over the possibility of tragedy. Instead of the identifying emotions of pity and fear, he enforces a detached critical awareness. The dramatic impact of the play is quite shocking and Parker has intended that it should be. No one imagined on that fatal night the Miami Showband was returning home late from a performance, in Northern Ireland, that they would meet such a horrific end to their lives. There may be mixed messages in *Catchpenny Twist*, as Elmer Andrews suggests, but Parker's own thoughts on what a play can or should do are fully realised as they are thrown out into the glare of the public arena where they are made ponderable: "There is an air of fatality about the play which suggests that no one from the north of Ireland remains immune from the situation, it becomes an insidious fact of life. We see in Roy and Martyn that their ideologically free existence is the most sterile illusion of all, for life without belief is without utopias, roots or a plan, without distance from itself and without a self-representation, and the disjointed episodic form of the play reflects the drifting emotion and the swirls and leaps of puppetry." (Andrew, 25. April/June 1989)

The "swirls and leaps of puppetry" are a part of the "compact of mutual impotence and sterility" which prevents the two communities from uniting in a common cultural bond, as much more is shared by them in cultural ties than either side cares to admit, especially the struggling working classes. What Parker has succeeded in doing is presenting the audience with an image of wholeness and one in which they can cease to pick over the entrails of the past and begin to hint at a vision of the future. The challenge is to find a belief in the future and to express it with due defiance in the teeth of whatever gory chaos may meanwhile prevail.

Spokesong had seven songs and *Catchpenny Twist* eleven. Parker felt that his next obvious step was to write a full musical to continue his very fruitful collaboration with Shaun Davey. He had expressed interest in trying to write about the situation in Northern Ireland that would transcend local boundaries and make connections with other parts of the world. The West Indies had fascinated Parker, as they were countries that had parallels and connections between their societies and Northern Ireland in the aftermath of colonialism. In contrast to the final scenes in *Catchpenny Twist*, Parker began a much lighter work in *Kingdom Come* (1977) that was written during the time of the second, unsuccessful, loyalist strike in Northern Ireland. Elaborating on the musical elements in his work and in collaboration with Shaun Davey, Parker produced the Irish-Caribbean musical that was designed for the King's Head Theatre in London.

This unlikely choice of an Irish-Caribbean musical grew from Parker's fascination with the culture of the West Indies and his discovery that the Caribbean island, Montserrat, had an Irish connection. The island was lightly re-imagined by Parker to provide the setting for *Kingdom Come*.

Montserrat's first European visitor was Christopher Columbus in 1493 who named the island after a mountain in Spain and later colonised by British and Irish settlers fleeing religious persecution. They brought their black slaves and indentured servants with them from St. Kitts in 1632. The island became a British crown colony in 1783.

As a consequence, the population of Montserrat today is comprised mostly of black people with Irish names, Irish accents, a government house with a large shamrock over it and a lady with an Irish harp adorning the Montserrat postage stamp. All of this 'tickled' Parker's imagination. More importantly, it was the island's political situation, as an English crown colony with an English governor, which placed it in many respects alongside the political establishment in Northern Ireland during the1970s.

Kingdom Come is an attempt to look at colonialism in an unexpected way. It was fuelled by the second loyalist strike of 1977 that failed because the ordinary people of Belfast, and the country as a whole, had heroically resisted the demagoguery and the bullying tactics that were used at the time. The failure led to a sense of hope and optimism in the general population and it was this feeling that Parker wanted to celebrate in his play.

Macalla is a fictitious island that has all the features of Irish society, a post-colonial society with racial and religious prejudice which Parker would "send up ... and turn into a kind of silly farce in which every sort of fanatical obsession that you get in places like this would be parodied and mocked. The least regarded person in society, the servant, the one who is tramped on by everyone else, would end up taking over the Island, and rule it." (Parker, 1978). Macalla Island's post-colonial rulers are monomaniacs, obsessive political figures blinkered by their own obsessions, who lose their sense of humanity in pursuing very limited and fanatical ends.

Kingdom Come could be read as an allegory, but Parker felt that allegory was overstating his intentions, as he considered it to be a play that should be a light-hearted evening where the audience could laugh at their prejudices rather than an abrasive examination of their differences. Parker has described his writing as "performing on a high wire ... There are so many ways in which you can fall off and I have been aware of treading a delicate line because, after all, I am using very volatile material. The most volatile issues in our society are probably race and the Irish question and I was hoping that I could steer a course in the middle of those issues which would not cause offence, but at the same time would give people something to think about." (Parker, 1978)

In *Spokesong* and *Catchpenny Twist* the songs were used to parody different styles of songwriting. In *Kingdom Come* the characters have a range of songs, many of which are musical jokes, which complement the verbal jokes within diverse styles: reggae, calypso, jigs, reels and Irish-Caribbean rhythms. Each character sings in a style most suited to his or her obsession or background. Miss Dunwoody, an Anglo-Irish woman, sings in an upper-class style reminiscent of Nöel Coward, while the Irish Macallan priest, Father O'Prey, parodies Irish folk music.

Lyrics, Parker once remarked, "are what I write on the back of a cigarette packet when I go to bed. I do them for relaxation." Shaun Davey, the composer for *Catchpenny Twist* and *Kingdom Come*, recalls that Parker's comments to an over-intense and immature composer may have been intended as a timely deflation of serious expectations. It seemed a curious statement from Parker, as he revered the songs of Cole Porter and Irving Berlin and the craft that went into them, but a statement from a modest man who had a wry habit of self-effacement. Davey and Parker took great delight in the lyrics for *Kingdom Come*:

Bit late in the day to explain
Respectfully I remain
Lying on a rumpled bedstead
Staring at an ashen sky
Flotsam dropped off by the ebb tide
Crossmaglen and hope to die.

Lenore je t'adore

I remember each item you wore
When you took off your jumper
Outside Kuala Lumpur
A typhoon engulfed Singapore. (47)

There are many different musical styles in *Kingdom Come* but Davey admits that he wished he could have included more traditional Irish music and not just 'ceili' music. The audience is taken by surprise by the switching of styles in keeping with the characters in the play and the music is in effect an affectionate pastiche as revealed in the opening Rumba, which has all the deftness and playful invention of the great American songwriters:

Macalla
You can take your girl to a gala
Macalla
You can hear a steel band play Mahler
though it may not be up to La Scala
It possesses a je ne sais qual-
ity ever so faintly outré
Follow me down to Vahalla
It's like living a part in a play. (3)

Music in *Kingdom Come* is used to reinforce character, especially the archetypes of the Irish priest, the Black police chief and Miss Dunwoody, the doughty descendant of the old English aristocracy. Teresa, the downtrodden, priest-ridden serving maid, is coerced into taking the lead role in the island's musical gala celebration of its history. Her transition, from a hitherto virtually mute character, is unexpected and dramatic and it is at this point that Parker placed his faith in the power of music to speak clearly and with unquestionable sincerity.

When Macalla's Protestant island patriots call for a constitutional Universal Declaration of Independence, the Black Republicans demand that the British go home. The dialogue is a quick-fire miscellany of barbed innuendoes critical of colonialism. Parker alludes to the mis-management of Northern Ireland and aligns it with similar Caribbean dissatisfaction that will culminate in a visit by the Queen. There are several minor plots in which all the parties connive against each other, but in effect, they all work towards the same goal that is the acceptance and instalment of their particular ideology.

A festival on the island celebrates the 300th anniversary of the settlement of Macalla, and a festival committee assembles on the verandah of a hotel, ostensibly to plan the show, and to hatch fractional plots for an anniversary coup. Intrigue festers and old party member, Pyecraft, admits to having British parliamentary connections. The Black police chief is in league with Miss Dunwoody, a figurehead of the Protestant ascendancy, while a Black newspaper editor is in league with a judge's daughter, and a Republican priest with an island girl, Teresa. By means of bombings, shootings, and mass poisoning, each group hopes to wipe out the opposition. An unstressed parallel can be drawn with Irish history as the island is divided into these uneasy factions that unfurl in the gentlest way, highlighting Anglo-Irish Imperialism on the Caribbean island.

The message in *Kingdom Come* is, according to Conor Cruise O'Brien, strong, valid and urgent. The critics in London were evenly divided in their appraisal of the play, but O'Brien is strident in his defence of it: "It is a play about the liberation of a people, but it is not about their liberation in the sense in which that term is used by those who use it most; quite the contrary. It is about the liberation of the people of Northern Ireland from their supposed liberators—the IRA in the case of the Catholics—and from their supposed defenders—the sectarian paramilitary in the case of the Protestants." (O'Brien, 1978)

Kingdom Come actually explores a turning point in the history of Northern Ireland, according to O'Brien. The failure of the second loyalist strike in Northern Ireland on 3 May, 1977, revealed the failure of the mass of Protestant workers to follow the lead of the Reverend Ian Paisley. The Catholic population's march of the Peace Women defied IRA intimidation, as they went out of the Catholic and into the Protestant ghetto. Most writing about the Northern Ireland tragedy has wilted under the sheer sordid ugliness of murder and counter-murder in dark wet streets. By transporting Northern Ireland to another geographical location, the players and the audience in *Kingdom Come* have become liberated from the emotional dominance of the rival fanatics.

Michael Billington, writing for the *Guardian*, found confusion and a sense of impenetrability in *Kingdom Come*: "The whole concept is fundamentally flawed; for in attempting to give us an Irish political allegory in the context of a Caribbean Island's quest for identity, Mr. Parker has managed to make a confusing situation almost wholly impenetrable ... Clearly Mr. Parker is trying, as in *Spokesong*, to approach the Irish problem through comedy and music, but here the basic conceit is just too extravagant. It is never clear why the black Macallans should be involved in the internal struggles of the whites, and how Mr. Parker reconciles his apolitical, plague-on-both-your houses attitude to the Irish problem with its apparent endorsement of black political power." (Billington, 1978) Billington enjoyed Shaun Davey's music and admits to being never bored!

The relationship of *Kingdom Come* to Northern Ireland's troubles may not be clear to those who know Northern Ireland by report only, and in the final song, 'Jubilio', Teresa, an uneducated woman, who has been used as a tool by the terrorists, sings of liberation. Before us on stage is baffled intelligence, dis-embaffling itself as a great, moving, turning point in the life of a person or community. Parker wanted his play to be performed in Ireland and Montserrat: "I don't know if there's even a theatre in Montserrat, I wouldn't think so. I did meet a chap from Montserrat who came to one of the previews; he was a very charming, young black man called Wendell O'Flaherty and he seemed to enjoy it very much. I asked him if he thought we could take it to Montserrat and he was a bit dubious." (Allen, 1987)

Written and first performed in Dublin, *Nightshade* (1980) baffled Irish critics who questioned Parker as a serious playwright, despite the success of his work for the theatre, television and radio. The British were equally confused by *Nightshade* as critics and audiences could not dissociate the tragedy that surrounds death and the humour that surrounds bereavement. The play has very serious undertones and Parker humorously, if not wickedly, juggles the complexities of death by warping the realism that engulfs our perception of it, to get, as he describes it, to a spiritual truth: "It was a play in which I had to face up to the monsters and phantoms in my mind, the realisation that you're going to die. I nearly died when I was nineteen but it didn't enter my consciousness. In my thirties the fact that I was going to die hit me, and I wanted to deal with that. Death in Ireland is frequently part of the farce of life." (Allen, 1987) In Belfast, Parker's black humour is keenly understood.

Nightshade is a mixture of experiment, inventiveness, wit, theatricality, obscure motifs and elements that are deeply moving, in a work that is ostensibly concerned with our approach to death and its rituals. It is a highly complex play as there is no story that is told in sequence and its meaning cannot be easily grasped. The play is also a comedy in which the jokes, both verbal and visual, bubble merrily from what in essence is deepest gloom. The action offers profound questions about the relationships between the living and the dying and raises more questions about whether the physical act of dying really has much to do with death itself. These themes reveal some of the complexity of *Nightshade*, as it becomes a surrealistic amalgam of parable and reality, of the prosaic and the scarcely imaginable, and of the comic and the profoundly sad.

Nightshade is a series of melodramatic events presented as deadpan irony. The surreal plot line is reinforced by the representational stage setting and by the exaggerated implausible relationships between the principal characters. Parker described it as "formalised and symmetrical, with the disproportion of a dream ... At its centre is a shiny black curtain, lustrously swagged and tucked, which can be drawn up to reveal what is— figuratively as well as literally—an inner stage. The action is fast and continuous, a constant traffic, the fitful opening and closing of possibilities ... The staging and lighting should be as magic as possible: discoveries, disappearances, transformations; one foot through the looking-glass, at least." (163)

It is more than likely that W.B. Yeats would have approved of Parker's stagecraft. His use of lighting, curtains, raised platforms, doors and walls to divide the main stage into various rooms and 'psychological spaces' recalls Yeats' experiments with the folding and unfolding of cloths and screens as a means of separating actions and places. The Plays for Dancers, by Yeats, most certainly contain all of these elements of stagecraft in the use of masks, cloths and screens that must only be used to symbolise or suggest. (McCracken, 71)

As Kathleen McCracken argues: "Parker's connection with Yeats is less firmly established than his relation with Synge as there are some formal and thematic continuities between their essentially different approaches to drama. The momentum in Yeats' plays often seems suspended because the action takes place within a fixed mythological or historical context. Parker's plays are made up of a series of brief and loosely connected episodes that usually take place in a contemporary setting, although his later plays delve into the historical past. The effect of this pattern at the close of *Nightshade* is to give a picture of the suspended animation of modern life and a terrifying pastiche of the living end. Irony in Yeats' plays is also dependent upon the mythological or historical context, and in a similar manner the melodramatic surface of *Nightshade*, and the ironies which arise out of it, are based largely on Biblical or folkloric allusions." (McCracken, 72)

The dark mysterious atmosphere throughout *Nightshade* is in keeping with the theme of magic and transformation. Underneath the verbal wit and comic action there is a disconcerting undercurrent of violence and psychological disruption. Parker collates fairytale, mystery story and political satire and exploits the potential for melodrama inherent in each genre, and the result is a parable of contemporary society. *Nightshade* examines the struggles of coming to terms with death and the terrible consequences of avoiding it. John Quinn, a bereaved mortician, is practicing conjuring tricks in his spare time. The mortuary workers are on strike and his business faces takeover. Quinn's wife, Agnes, has recently died, a fact that he conceals from his daughter. The 'performing acts', by Quinn, are an essential ingredient in the play and hearken back to Parker's own conjuring tricks that he recalls in his John Malone Memorial Lecture.

In *Nightshade* we can distinguish two functions of Quinn's illusions: the first is deliberately to mystify and hide the truth from view to create ideological illusion by which ideas and images mask the truth of the world: the second is to present how the artist works with illusion. "What Stewart Parker urges is a vigilant scrutiny of our illusory representation projects and fantasies so that whatever is negative and alienating can be deconstructed and unmasked." (Kennedy, 1987)

Quinn's magic show offers an illusion about death as he thrusts his ornamental sword into a box containing his daughter Delia; the audience hears Delia scream, as blood spurts from the box; Delia reappears and tap dances offstage. "This initial scene may be regarded as a paradigm of the play, where apparently serious references and events are deliberately undercut by a surprising and often comic reversal. In these instances, reality is generally held at bay by an overlay of fantasy that comes suddenly to the fore and allows the melodramatic aspect of the play to achieve its full dramatic impact." (McCracken, 70)

Quinn's magic show offers people an illusion about death as he sets out to satisfy the demand for painless loss. Death is turned into big business as a mechanical routine in which the wishes of his employees, their relatives and the deceased are largely ignored. Quinn's kind of funeral is simply an extension of the cheap tricks he performs at children's parties in which "miracles can be made to happen" in the "efficient disposition of the deceased":

> QUINN: You don't need me to tell you people ... miracles can be made to happen. The impossible takes a little time, that's all. One year in this case. We showed them how—matchless ... (he opens his matchbox again, but this time pulls a red handkerchief out of it) that's the word for it. Double your fleet of motors. Triple your turnover. A new branch in the New Year, how do we do it? Business sense. Hard graft. Teamwork—a performance not to be sneezed at, in this day and age. With the country in rags and tatters all around us—and plenty of other firms in the soup. (164)

In Parker's theatricality there is a crucial difference between Quinn the magician, giving the illusion and appearance of truth, and the playwright who gives truth in the pleasant disguise of illusion. Ironically, in the end it is the spirit-world that defeats the materialist Quinn as he tries to hide from the facts of his wife's disappearance and from the fact that she couldn't stand the "smell of white lilies and dark heavy clothes. Polished wood and sanctity and guilt and grief, the smog of the funeral industry." (193) The ghost of Agnes returns to haunt Quinn in the end, tormenting him and ultimately destroying him. The garden she had nurtured becomes "rat infested ... On account of Agnes being dead you see. It's a jungle now, that garden. A nest of rats down by the Rowan tree ... It was her creation that garden. It's a wild jungle now. I haven't set foot in it since she died, except that night with her ashes." (244)

Delia, Quinn's daughter, rewrites two stories which give an ironic perspective on his unholy enterprise. Her version of *The Sleeping Beauty* does not have its traditional happy ending as her dithery prince shuffles in, covered in mud and smelling of horse.

His magic kiss is ineffectual in reversing the fact of death. Delia's speech is an exclamation that humanity no longer knows how to live or die properly:

> DELIA: We are the tribe, which has lost the knowledge of how to die. In the boundless abundance by which we act, this supreme skill has somehow been misled. Yet this one action—which we all dread—is the only one that's forced upon us without exception. And we do it in shame and in confusion. Other tribes, who knew much less, at least knew this. They died with conviction and finesse. But we are entirely in the dark ... For a person begins to die at the moment of birth. So dying is an action that we perform throughout our lives. And so—at the heart's core—we are the tribe that has lost the knowledge of how to live. (232)

Since Quinn's humanity does not absorb Parker so intimately as Frank's did in *Spokesong*, the subjectivist emphasis of the earlier play is tilted to the other objectivist extreme in *Nightshade*'s heartless puppetry. Elmer Andrews contends "the continued disjunction between subject and object means that we continue to miss the constant Brechtian kind of insight into the incongruities and contradictions of human motive. The irony is too dispassionate to produce ambivalence and lest we miss the point Delia spells it out for us in the tribe, which has lost the knowledge of how to die. *Nightshade* works reflexively as it invites us to ponder our own life and death." (Andrews, April-June 1989)

In working his "alchemy of pleasure and enlightenment" on the stage, Parker's plays lie somewhere between the models of Yeats and Synge. He suggests that if his work belongs to any tradition it is that of the "venerable Anglo-Irish tradition of comedy of manners, stretching from Congreve and Farquhar through Sheridan and Goldsmith to Wilde and beyond." (*Ibid*) It is for this reason that Parker found melodrama an appealing and an exact vehicle to convey his ideas. The result is an independent, newly invented drama, which although not entirely dissociated from the stage craft of the Irish Revival, redirects the strengths of that theatrical tradition in order to entertain.

Pratt's Fall, Parker's sixth major play, was first produced at Glasgow's Tron Theatre in 1981. His inspiration for *Pratt's Fall* goes back to his childhood in east Belfast, where as an infant, he was baptised in the shipyard parish of St. Brendan's, Church of Ireland. He grew up knowing Brendan was called 'the navigator' because he was the seafaring hero of the golden age of Irish monastic culture. A medieval map, pre-dating Columbus' discovery of America by six centuries, is believed to be the work of Brendan. The period between the fifth and ninth centuries AD, the Dark Ages in most of Europe, was when the wandering saints and scholars carried the beacon of their arts and letters from Clonmacnoise, Kells, Bangor, Iona, Britain and across the whole known world.

The annal 'The Voyage of Saint Brendan' (c. 800 AD) describes the saint's voyage westward in an oxhide curragh to the Land Promised of the Saints. (In 1976 Tim Severin reconstructed a medieval curragh and successfully sailed from Brandon Creek in County Kerry to Newfoundland, thus adding to the body of scientific evidence for the Irish discovery of America.) In *Pratt's Fall* the new scientific discovery rests on the recent discovery of the Brendan Map that Parker weaves into the central plot of the play. Map-making is a central metaphor: "there is no such thing as an absolutely perfect map ... a map is just one person's picture of the world as he sees it at the time ... Your map and mine might look like different planets, if we were to compare them." (*Pratt's Fall*, 1981)

Parker gives precise, detailed descriptions for the stage setting for *Pratt's Fall*: "The time is the present, and the place sometimes the Map Room of a major metropolitan library and at other times a room in a flat, a monastery library, a conference hall stage, and an office in a map-publishing firm ... A decorative arch curves above this, connecting the two columns, with the words IMAGO

MUNDI carved into it. In the centre of the space under the arch and above the books is a large reproduction antique clock face, showing ten to twelve; the rest of the space around this is filled with a frieze imitating the engravings on early printed charts, something like the frontispiece of William Blaeu's The Light Of Navigation, 1612." (249)

The play is written in two parts, 'Hesperides' and 'Bondage'. George Mahoney reflects on the future of visionary hope and dynamic energy in the Western. He attempts to change the world with the aid of a bogus map to rewrite history and to persuade us that America was discovered by the ninth century monks of Ardfert. He hopes thus to reactivate man's spirituality in a material world by persuading him to reconsider the miracle of faith which impelled the early missionary adventures.

In his John Malone lecture, Parker discussed Johan Huizinga's theories of 'Play' and its influence on his work. This influence is at work in Spokesong and emerges, even more powerfully, in Pratt's Fall. The play is a semiotic force which interrogates and disrupts given identities, stable meanings and institutions with a view to producing a new human subject, what Parker calls a "workable model of wholeness". Reality, meanings and ideas, the ways we experience the world, are dependent on certain shared forms of social consciousness and systems of signification. What meanings are available to us depend on what language or, as in Pratt's Fall, what 'map' is shared in the first place.

In the opening monologue Godfrey Dudley introduces the audience to Mahoney as someone "lusting as always for somebody rash and ill-advised to create an incident, and let's give George his due, he treated the whole bunch of us to a sort of downright bloody major international sensation of sorts, him and his map". (252) This monologue is a reverie in the mind of Godfrey, a devoted administrator who is trying to rehearse his wedding speech and wondering if his friend George Mahoney will attend the wedding.

Mahoney believes in belief for its own sake and enjoys

launching into uncharted territory of either the mind or emotions. He once knew Victoria Pratt, the cartographer, who had followed the facts and scientific evidence dispassionately, wherever they might lead, until she met George. Mahoney's claim to have found the map to prove that Saint Brendan sailed the Atlantic, seems to convince the scrupulous Victoria Pratt of its authenticity. Parker poses several questions in the play: should we charter our journey through life on faith or on facts or go into unmapped territory or travel by way of prearranged package tours however adventurous these may sound? David Nowland contends that: "The script is too intellectually discursive to provide emotional satisfaction in the personal struggle between Mahoney and Pratt ... a struggle that can also be seen as one between Celt and Anglo-Saxon." (Nowland, 10)

> GODFREY: But then all beliefs are cuckoo if you are looking in from the outside. Though some of you here today are very deft in that regard. You can shuffle the whole pack without dropping a card. I myself have never really acquired the knack somehow. What I find is—the moment somebody else expounds a point of view, which I share ... my belief in it begins to crumble. I've lost any little beliefs I ever had that way. (264)

With the aid of a bogus map, Mahoney wants to re-write history, to persuade us that America was discovered by the ninth-century monks of Ardfert. What Godfrey finds intriguing about Mahoney is his belief in mystery and his opposition to the fixity and closure of knowledge: "The prospect of a world that's fully known. No more hidden valleys, no more dark interiors. Just what's here, what's on the map? The end of adventure. The death of all the planet's possibilities." (288)

Victoria Pratt acknowledges that it is beliefs which govern the world, and not facts, and her wounded pride in the discovery that Mahoney's map is a fake makes him a failed 'Playboy of the Western World'. Mahoney's project, like Christy Mahon's fantasy of killing his father, in Synge's *The Playboy of the Western*

World, begins in illusion. Despite her mistake, Victoria has no desire, never mind the courage, to change her world. Even more conventionalised than Synge's Pegeen, Victoria rejects her Playboy with not the slightest sense of loss. *Pratt's Fall* brought some advance in Parker's effort to find a way to bring individual will and the objective world into a dialectical relationship with each other.

Lost Belongings (1987) adapts the Deirdre of the Sorrows myth into a modern setting. The six-part series for television was also an exorcism of Parker's Belfast roots in much the same way that *Over the Bridge* was for Thompson but it does not evoke the raw emotions found in the earlier playwright's work. Television drama also provided a means of production for new work, as Parker stated: "I'm mulling over the feasibility of a trilogy of films set in Ulster during the last fourteen years. What has happened is that various and sundry ideas have suddenly grouped themselves together in my mind. The three films have different characters, different milieus and tone of voice, but they all deal with individuals whose lives are affected by the large events in which they are trying to live. And taken together, they should present a composite picture of sorts, a summation of the Northern Irish seventies. The sort of trilogy I have in mind is the 'Wajda' trilogy about wartime Poland." (Parker, 1987)

Lost Belongings weaves a mythic tale into late twentieth-century Ireland. It would be easy to ridicule the television work without reference to its ideological content. Longes mac n-Uislenn (The Exile of the Sons of Uisliu) is a short narrative in old Irish dating from the eighth or ninth-century AD. It is the earliest extant version of a tale from Irish mythology that is known in more prettified and sentimental folklore renditions as Deirdre Of The Sorrows: "The wife of the storyteller in the Ulster court is big with child, and when the foetus screams in her womb the court druid prophesies that she will be a girl-child called Deirdre, whose great beauty will bring catastrophe upon Ulster. As soon as the child is born, the King of Ulster, Connor, decrees that she is to be reared in seclusion for his own delectation. She grows not only lovely but also highly-spirited as is evident from her comment upon seeing her foster-father skin a calf in the snow while a nearby raven sips at the calf's blood: 'I could well desire a man with hair as black as that raven, cheeks as red as blood, and a body as white as the snow.' Such a man is soon found, singing on the rampart. He and his two brothers sing so sweetly that 'every cow or animal that heard them gave them two-thirds more milk.' They are the three sons of Uisliu, and the one Deirdre falls for is the eldest one, Noisiu. She demands that he take her away with him.

"The three brothers are forced to flee into exile with Deirdre, to escape from the jealous and vengeful rage of Connor. They live for a while in Scotland and in due course, Connor is prevailed upon to pardon them, to free them from the pains and perils of exile, to forgive and forget, and to send his trusty henchman Fergus as a surety of safe passage home. The sons of Uisliu return to Ulster, along with Deirdre ... and are promptly slaughtered by Connor's minions in an act of treachery, which precipitates civil war in the Province. Deirdre is held captive for a year by Connor. During that time, she never smiled, never ate properly nor slept either, nor raised up her knees. Eventually, whilst out riding in a chariot one day, seated next to Connor, she sees a large boulder up ahead. She let her head be driven against the rock and smashed it into pieces, and she was dead." (Kinsella, 1969)

A modern-day audience would be unaware of the source of the myth, but Parker was convinced that the story was timeless as it contained a universal resonance that linked the six parts of *Lost Belongings*. The plot is complex in an effort to create characters that encapsulate often contradictory factors, which shape loyalties and identity in Northern Ireland. Deirdre is at once both Catholic and Protestant but her own illegitimacy makes her a member of neither community.

Lost Belongings is set in 1980 and the events Parker states are not autobiographical: "I have been a resident of Belfast, my native city up until 1978. Having lived there for a total of thirty-one years, I feel entitled to go on writing about it indefinitely. However, the fabric of time and place and incident is very intricate and specific in these stories, so that each additional year away felt like another bandage wound around my writing hand. I wasn't living there, for example when the Maze hunger strikers died in 1981. I wasn't living there when the Anglo-Irish Agreement was signed at Hillsborough in 1985. I would not have felt comfortable trying to express how events such as those impinged on the lives of these particular characters. At any rate, drama needs some measure of distance to achieve any kind of coherence. If the distance can't be emotional, then it has to be historical. There is by now a widespread feeling throughout Britain that Northern Ireland is the black hole of British politics, into which normal principles, issues and panaceas disappear without trace. Because the inter-communal conflict has so many interlocking elements: nationalist, religious, colonial, ethnic, class, economic the situation presents a seemingly intractable challenge to democratic solutions. The one certainty is that it will not go away." (Parker, 1987)

Lost Belongings is a compelling adaptation of the Deirdre myth and a commentary on present-day Northern Ireland. Parker imbues Deirdre with a sensitivity and an artistic nature beyond the terms of the myth. After her uncle, Roy Connell, makes another sexual advance, Deirdre is seen crying and writing on toilet paper, but she flushes away what she had written before her uncle could find it. Parker explained this as the primal artistic impulse, writing because she has to, but with no hope of an audience.

"I keep a flower that burns in me and I keep a flame that blooms in me, and it won't be plucked and it won't be put out, not by his hands pawing me and his boozy breath deafening me." This introduces the primary image of fire representing creativity, or the life fire that blooms in Deirdre, which is also seen as destructive. Deirdre is a child of fire; as a baby she was rescued from the blaze that consumed her parents. Later in life Deirdre literally sets herself ablaze when she can no longer tolerate her uncle's cruel captivity. This death-fire image fulfils the dictates of the myth as Fergus burned Emain Macha, the sacred centre of Ulster, as retaliation when Connor killed the sons of Uisliu. These images of life-fire and death-fire are central to the Deirdre of the Sorrows myth and permeate *Lost Belongings*.

Parker exercises his historian's mind, as well as his experience, in writing several major works for the theatre, television and radio over a fifteen-year period and reveals his flexible talent and a poetic sensibility in many areas of the theatre. He became a man of the theatre, not only in producing scripts, but also in his understanding of the actor's and designer's process in creating a composite work of art. A thread began to weave its way from *Spokesong*, which began his major plays for the theatre, and completed the cycle in his final play *Pentecost*. The struggle to deal with the inner self is paramount in Parker's work and is fully realised in his final three plays. In each of the plays he wrestles with the past to try to find coherence in the complex web of opposing nationalities, which is Ulster, and places the plays in the centre of the Anglo-Irish tradition with its creative distancing and cool remove. It is within this tradition that Parker found his greatest articulation in *Three Plays for Ireland*, which is the subject of the following chapter.

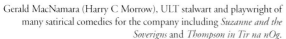

An unkown ULT production featuring Harry Morrow (right seated) and Fred Morrow (right standing).

The Ulster Literary Theatre in an unknown production featuring Harry Morrow (right seated) and Fred Morrow (right standing). The writers gathered around the ULT often experienced a sense of cultural inferiority believing that their work had been sidelined and undervalued.

Gerald MacNamara (Harry C Morrow), ULT stalwart and playwright of many satirical comedies for the company including *Suzanne and the Soverigns* and *Thompson in Tir na nOg.*

Sam Thompson with fellow playwright Joseph Tomelty. As a pivotal figure in the development of modern Irish drama, Thompson presented an authentic urban voice on the stage in Belfast.

Sam Thompson with his son, Warren.

Stewart Parker, typically cigar in hand. Parker wrote from the inside of the Protestant heart and mind and from this position he could afford a black and scabrous humour about his own tribe.

Sean Kearns (l) and Sean Caffrey (r) in a Lyric Players Theatre's production of *Spokesong*. Parker's play views the nature of violence in Northern Ireland in such a way as to take the audience completely by surprise.

Stewart Parker with the original cast of *Kingdom Come*. The unlikely choice of an Irish-Caribbean musical grew from Parker's fascination with the West Indies and his discovery that the Caribbean island, Montserrat, had an Irish connection.

Stella McCusker in *Kingdom Come*. Jimmy Greene (l) Chris Barett (r).

Lalor Roddy in a scene from Gary Mitchell's *As The Beast Sleeps*.

Gary Mitchell. Mitchell's claustrophic imaginative landscape portrays a contemporary Northern Protestant experience where every gesture is questioned and every word carefully weighed.

From left to right: Robert Donovan, Sean Kearnes, Colm Convey, Mark McCrory in *As the Beast Sleeps*.

Carol Scanlon (r) Marie Jones (c) Brenda Winters (l) in Charabanc Theatre's *Lay Up Your Ends*.

Conleth Hill (l) and Sean Campion (r) in Marie Jones' *Stones in His Pockets*.

Dan Gordon, as Kenneth McAllister, in *A Night in November*. Jones' play is an exploration of the cultural assumption of northern Protestantism.

CHAPTER FOUR

Three Plays for Ireland

The triptych *Three Plays for Ireland* begins with *Northern Star* and the slightly insane idea that the best way to write a play about Henry Joy McCracken is in the styles of the great Irish playwrights George Farquhar and Samuel Beckett. *Northern Star* was conceived many years before his return to Belfast in 1969 from America and was his first play to receive its premiere at the Lyric Theatre, Belfast, in 1984. Events that had taken place in the US during the late 1960s had had a profound effect on Parker's later career as a dramatist. He said he conceived the play while living in the United States where he engaged in protests against Vietnam and segregation. In 1967, while teaching at Cornell, Parker began drafts of his play about Henry Joy McCracken and the failed rebellion of 1798. As a liberal, who later became a member of the newly formed Alliance Party, Parker had a political affinity with the ideals of the United Irishmen.

In the introduction to his *Three Plays for Ireland* Parker writes: "So far as the 'real' characters are concerned, they have been drawn from the marginalia of the historical record rather than its main plot. Henry Joy McCracken was a minor figure in the '98

Rising in Ireland; not enough is known about him (*Northern Star*). Dion Boucicault was unarguably a major force in the Victorian theatre ... rather more than enough is known about him (*Heavenly Bodies*). The first play employs pastiche as a strategy, and the second one a kind of collage; the third play is written in a form of heightened realism (*Pentecost*)." (Parker 9, 1989)

Parker had been studying the historical figure of Henry Joy McCracken over many years and was looking for a context in which to place him in contemporary Northern Ireland. The present state of Ireland bears so strongly on the past in the play that in delineating the one we seem to portray the character of both. A constant tension is maintained between the past in the play and the events surrounding McCracken's life and the images of him that have been passed down through history. The play is not a naturalistic narrative of McCracken's life, but a theatrical entertainment that constantly reminds the audience that it is watching a performance, in Belfast, in the present. Writing the play in the styles of seven Irish playwrights emphasises this theatricality.

History, said Joyce's Stephen Dedalus, "is a nightmare from which I am trying to wake". In *Northern Star* Parker embraces history as a hermetic prison and a potent metaphor. There is a dazzling Joycean structure in the play and virtuosic delight as serious issues are handled comically as Parker parodies everything, from the ingenious paradoxes of Oscar Wilde, to the incantatory rhetoric of J.M. Synge. There is a clear, serious purpose behind the literary devices, which suggest Ireland can achieve unity only by acknowledging its plurality. The best way to escape from the prison of the past lies in celebrating art and reason, rather than mythologising violence.

Northern Star shares with *Heavenly Bodies* and *Pentecost* the figure of a ghost, the "uncomplicated souls" as Parker calls them: the Phantom Bride in *Northern Star*, the Phantom Fiddler in *Heavenly Bodies* and the ghost of Lily Mathews in *Pentecost*. The Phantom Bride is a central symbol in *Northern Star*, and as a ghost from the past, she returns to haunt McCracken during the hours before his martyrdom. The tradition of Irish political martyrdom is personified in McCracken as a form of sacrifice for Mother Ireland and is exemplified in Yeats' *Cathleen Ni Houlihan* and the *Shan Van Vocht* (the short-lived Irish Nationalist literary magazine from 1886-1889). Through the images of phantoms and ghosts we see how the archaeological sense of a continuous past, while inspired by the desire of a community for security, continuity and identity, can be hopelessly mystifying and reactionary. This can also contribute to a social order that, in itself, encourages a tragic fatalism and political stagnation.

The rebellion of 1798 might have been a revolution, according to Seamus Deane. To call it a rebellion reminds us of the defeat of revolutionary principles that lay at its heart: "But 1798 is not over yet, we are still the inheritors and victims of that moment when the possibility of an enlightened future was crushed by a government and a system devoted to the preservation of sectarian privilege and to the repression of the new languages of freedom, equality, citizenship and justice ... The rebellion has been claimed as a Protestant triumph over a Catholic conspiracy and as a heroic Catholic rebellion against Protestant and British despotism. It was neither. It still has to be fought, for the thirty thousand who died in that fateful year still await their proper commemoration. It is clearer than ever now that the principles of secular republicanism, most memorably formulated by Wolfe Tone, are the most effective antidote to the internecine illnesses which have plagued this island for too long." (Deane, 1998)

Discriminatory laws had been enforced against Presbyterians as well as Catholics throughout the eighteenth century. Presbyterians, who had played a major role in the defeat of the Catholic James II, continued to feel excluded from public life, which was dominated by the Anglicans. Presbyterians, therefore, were aligned in many respects with the Catholic population that had been completely disenfranchised. In many areas of Ulster, the Presbyterians formed a majority of the population and had little sympathy for their Catholic neighbours. Late into the century the Catholic population was no longer considered a threat by the Presbyterians and, in many respects, shared the same conditions both socially and economically. Many radical Protestants were now prepared to accept the Catholics, as they no longer posed a threat to them, in their attempts to subvert the system of privilege upon which the Protestant, Anglican ascendancy rested.

Anglo-Irish, and the way it came to be applied to Irish-born Protestants, expresses the schizophrenia that was their natural condition. It was a culture in suspension between two other irreconcilable cultures, the parent English, and the native Irish, in an imbalanced condition which involved ingenious strategies for survival and adaptation, peculiarly suited to both politics and the stage. In this condition there is always a struggle towards a wholeness of expression and towards a harmonising of divided allegiances. Parker inherited the great gifts of Anglo-Irish theatricality as well as this journey towards the resolution of these differences.

Theobald Wolfe Tone founded the Society of United Irishmen on 14 October, 1792 in Belfast. He was encouraged by the French revolutionaries to attempt to achieve by force what he had failed to achieve by constitutional agitation. Tone's declared aims were: "To subvert the tyranny of our execrable government, to break the connection with England ... and assert the independence of my country—these were my objects. To unite the whole people of Ireland ... to substitute the common name of Irishman, in place of the denominations of Protestant, Catholic and Dissenter— these were my means."

There has been a tendency to exaggerate the extent of rapprochement between Catholics and Protestants in 1798. The United Irish movement was dictated by expediency as much as by enlightenment and, for many, bigotry was laid aside rather than abandoned. It was after a clash between the Protestant Peep O'Day Boys and the Catholic Defenders that the Orange Order was founded on 21 September, 1795. Instead of uniting Irishmen, as the Presbyterian radicals had hoped during the late 1790s, the Peep O'Day Boys and the Orange Order left them more bitterly divided than ever.

The title of the play *Northern Star* is derived from the newspaper, *The Northern Star*, which was published in Belfast from January 1792 to 1797. It was a paper that could always be relied upon to explain and rationalise the reverses and convulsions of events in Paris through the early 1790s. It supported the execution of King Louis, as did Wolfe Tone. On domestic issues it trod a more careful path beginning by advancing political reform and criticising the violent methods of the 'Defenders'. There was little trust between the communities in late eighteenth-century Ireland, even though men like McCracken and Tone believed they had found a means of uniting the disparate factions through the United Irishmen. There was no political trust and no attempt at raising the gates to Liberalism and Enlightenment, which had shaken the rest of Europe.

Ireland has remained entrenched in both the Nationalist and Unionist versions of the Irish past that was, according to Parker, "a profound sense of history as a nightmare from which it is impossible to awaken". (Parker, 1984) The Unionist view of the past could highlight the increasing social and libertarian advantages of incorporation in a modernising multi-racial British state, but so deep-rooted was the popular awareness of, and resistance to, the Irish Republic's claims on the six counties, that the myth of siege overwhelms any more progressive self-understanding. When Parker reads the past as a continuous present, he confirms what Irish people—both unionist and nationalist—feel about their differing histories.

The United Irishmen remained intellectually vibrant because they never flinched from facing the real question of politics and the creation of a society fit to live in. The decade of the 1790s was an extraordinary decade in Irish history. The opportunity presented itself to transcend the age-old sectarian, ethnic and political system rooted in sectarian privilege and to replace it with secular democratic politics founded on universal ideas of equality and justice. The United Irish project, which involved creating a secular republic and recasting political participation on inclusive lines, was deliberately blocked by the British state, which used weapons of sectarianism, military terror and the suppression of the Irish parliament, to defeat the United Irishmen.

The United Irishmen didn't understand the sectarian forces they were unleashing and Parker's Catholics and Defenders in *Northern Star* are just as sectarian as the Orangemen and share the responsibility for the carnage in the failed rebellion. In the play, McCracken is a necrophiliac who chooses death over life at the end of the first act as he turns from his living lover to embrace a ghost. Parker's interest in McCracken and his contemporary relevance in Ireland are at the centre of the Republican movement. McCracken was an idealist, influenced by the French Revolution, and in seeking help from the French he had hoped to erase the English from Ireland. The failure, which the play dramatises, is not just McCracken's personal failure, as a leader and a man, but also a wholesale critique of Republicanism through his personal weakness and his egotism. McCracken's susceptibility to the stranglehold of old ghosts, his self-immolating martyr-complex, his undeviating sense of tragic destiny and the inadequacy of his social and political analysis disqualify McCracken as a model of revolutionary leadership.

If McCracken had succeeded in his struggle with the United Irishmen, the history of Ireland would have taken a different path, but the birth of the new nation envisaged by McCracken and the United Irishmen had been 'botched':

MCCRACKEN: We never made a nation. Our brainchild. Stillborn. Our own fault. We botched the birth. So what if the English do bequeath us to one another some day? What then? When there's nobody else to blame except ourselves? (75)

[124]

McCracken fails because he does not have, at his disposal, an ideological perspective that can penetrate the realities of men's experience in his time and place. The play dramatises the Republican view of history as continuous, cyclical, and static, from an objective, critical standpoint. Such a view of history is motivated by the desire to create a sense of social integration: "The configuration of certain events in the past makes them notoriously susceptible to mythic accretion, and through this process, a communal set of images, a tradition, is precipitated whereby a social group can recollect itself and justify its actions in terms of a sanctified past." (Andrews 1989, July-September)

If the 1790s can be seen as the pivotal decade in the evolution of modern Ireland, then an honest and accurate understanding of it is not just of scholarly interest but has serious implications for current political and cultural thinking. It is precisely because of its enduring relevance that 1798 has never truly passed out of politics and into history. The United Irishmen's ideas did not die with the events of 1798; they are still potent, valid and unrealised.

The 'Continuous Past' is a stage direction given by Parker, and the view of history in the play is reflected in the character of Henry Joy McCracken as he awaits his fate after the collapse of the rebellion. The play presumes that Irish history is about certain events that are recurrent manifestations of an underlying pattern or theme. In Ireland the static view of history predominates in those who have been influenced by nationalist interpretations of the past. The Northern Unionist also has a vision of the past that highlights the repetitive, static quality of Irish experience.

Parker was searching to find a way to write an 'Ulster play': "If you tune into any moment of Ulster history, it gets immediately crowded with all the other moments, voices are coming at you from other decades and other centuries. There's no linear, orderly rational narration with a nice ending; it's all happening simultaneously, you start speaking about an event that happened in Derry last week and immediately voices of 1641 are clamouring to be heard. The voices that are heard do not form an orderly narrative in a convincing tone of voice. Tune into it any given moment from it and the wavelength soon grows crowded with a babble of voices from all other moments, up to, and including the present one. I have tried to accommodate this obstinate, crucial fact of life by eschewing any single style, and attempting instead, a wide range of theatrical ventriloquism emboldened by the knowledge that Henry Joy McCracken was a gifted mimic." (Parker, 1984)

Stewart Parker inherited the great gifts of Anglo-Irish theatricality as well as the journey towards the resolution of the differences. One of the many important things about his work is that he helped to restore the creative distancing and play of intelligence in contemporary theatre. In doing so, he connects directly with the Anglo-Irish tradition. Nowhere is this connection more specific than in *Northern Star*, where an Anglo-Irish sensibility is seen at full stretch in pursuit of a major Anglo-Irish preoccupation, a sense of identity in fractured culture, what Parker himself called "multiplying dualities: two islands (the British Isles), two Irelands, two Ulsters, two men fighting over a field". (Kilroy, 1998)

The outline of the play follows the rise and fall of the United Irishmen from the 'Mudlers' Debating Club' to the degradation of Kilmainham jail. The ensuing sectarian strife, which followed when Henry Joy McCracken, during the failed rising, found his army routed by a British retreat. Parker's fascination with the United Irishmen rests in his belief that during the late eighteenth century, Ireland had the chance of becoming united and independent as a result of the Enlightenment, which was sweeping across Europe.

Creative distancing is the mark of Anglo-Irish drama from George Farquhar to Samuel Beckett (O'Casey is the exception for reasons of background and personal temperament). For others, whether the subject-matter was English manners, Connemara myth-making, or the fiercely reduced circumstances of the figures on Beckett's stage, the style is a way of creating a distancing perspective. Parker gives two reasons for the employment of the seven different periods of Anglo-Irish drama in *Northern Star*; the first is in a programme note for the play's first production: "Ulster history refuses to offer any single, coherent story, any one convincing tone of voice. So the playwright resorts to multiple voices, a theatrical ventriloquism." (Whelan, 1998). The second reason is found at the beginning of the play itself as Mary Bodle and McCracken embrace the notion of the revolutionaries as actors and revolution as a staged event with McCracken in the lead role. The seven stages of the United Irishmen take on a Shakespearean unity and literally 'act out' the doomed uprising; its hopes, its courage and its failure. A deeply political writer, Parker writes his historical play out of the present tense of his own life, in which he suffered the contemporary tragedy of Northern Ireland.

Northern Star parodies seven styles of Irish drama from the eighteenth century to the present. Each relates to the story of the failed rebellion of 1798 and to the seven pre-ordained phases which McCracken must live through, each age has its own style: Innocence in the style of George Farquhar; Melodrama in the style of Dion Boucicault, as McCracken attempts to organise the United Irishmen to counteract the sectarian conflict in Armagh after the battle of the Diamond; Cleverness in the style of Oscar Wilde at the Belfast Harp Festival; Dialectics in the style of Shaw in the shape of a Shavian British officer searching for rebels and explaining in polished dialectic his rational Unionist views; Heroism in the style of John Millington Synge, as the United Irishmen take their oath on the side of Cave Hill; Knowledge in the style of Brendan Behan and Samuel Beckett, and Compromise in the style of Sean O'Casey. A dubious alliance exists between the United Irishmen and two blustering sectarian O'Caseyesque defenders. The prison scene in Kilmainham Jail draws on Behan's style leading to the failed United Irishmen's rising and the bleak Beckettian despair over its failure, and finally McCracken's execution.

There are profound differences between the drama of Protestant Anglo-Irish and the drama of what might be called Catholic, nationalist Ireland. This is another example of the division of the cultural history where theatrical tradition is, at the very least, in Parker's terms 'bifurcated'. The Anglo-Irish came first, dominating the English-speaking theatre from the eighteenth century to the early decades of the twentieth century. Anglo-Irish theatre is usually summed up in a familiar list: Farquhar, Sheridan, Goldsmith, Boucicault, Wilde, Shaw, Yeats, Synge and O'Casey with Beckett as an enlarged appendix. The drama of Catholic Ireland did not really exist before the twentieth century.

Prior to the 1890s there was no indigenous Irish theatre. The Irish theatre was created by Yeats and a group of largely Anglo-Irish writers and intellectuals. The social realism that so bothered Yeats continues to be a central ingredient of Irish drama today from the work of Synge to the plethora of Irish plays in London and New York in recent years. This is a highly verbal theatre, but as drama it has little of the cool remove from its subject matter, which is so typical of Anglo-Irish theatricality.

Each play in Parker's triptych manipulates form as a vehicle for content. *Northern Star* uses theatrical ventriloquism to re-examine the entire Republican mythology. The trick, according to Parker, was not to write a play in any one style but rather as a series of pastiches. As an ardent admirer of Joyce he believed that if Joyce could employ the entire nine centuries of English literature in one chapter of *Ulysses*, 'Oxen of the Sun', why shouldn't a playwright borrow the voices of his predecessors? (Carty, 1985) Joyce illustrated the literary history of the English language and Parker traces the history of Irish theatre.

Northern Star confronts the audience with a past that has been the source of present strife. The history of the failed rising has been the history of Ireland and, according to Parker, created an endless civil war in which there has never been a nation state.

The setting for the play is on the slopes of Cave Hill, a landmark known to the citizens of Belfast as it towers above the city, covered in a thick-forested hillside, with caves hewn out of basalt in the sharp escarpments. The opening scene follows the last night of McCracken's life in a half-derelict cottage on the slopes of Cave Hill, where he is recalling his political career and thinking over the rebellion and the slaughter of innocent men while his Catholic lover and their illegitimate child accompany him and wait for news of the ship that will take him to America.

Stage directions give meticulous details of the cottage and its surroundings with instruments placed at the forestage, which are played by the actors: a Lambeg drum (a Protestant symbol) and a Bodhrán (an Irish symbol). Members of the company, who may each play several roles in the action, play the instruments, each accompanied by the change of a hat, coat or wig in a style which reflects the deliberate anachronisms and historical shifts of the successive scenes. McCracken looks back on what went terribly wrong during the events of the rebellion and does so through a series of flashbacks which all follow the predestined seven ages of man. The play opens with McCracken's lover, Mary Bodle, singing a lullaby to their illegitimate child in the cottage where McCracken will spend his last night as a free man. McCracken begins to speak the lines, which open and close the play:

> MCCRACKEN: Citizens of Belfast, the story so far. I stand here before you on the gallows tree, condemned to die for your sake. I stand guilty of nurturing a brotherhood of affection between the Catholics of this town and my fellow Protestants. I stand guilty of cherishing the future happiness of our country above that of my insignificant self. I go willingly to my death in the true faith of a Presbyterian, confident in the blind belief that you will all unite together in freedom ... (14-15)

McCracken is about to face the gallows and according to an eyewitness account: "He stood for a moment beneath the gallows, his eyes following the retreating figure of his beloved sister, he then turned his gaze upon the crowd and seemed as if he would address them. Hoarse orders were given by the officers, the troops moved about, the people murmured, a horrible confusion ensued and in a minute or so the handsome figure was dangling at a rope's end." (Parker, 1984)

The play develops through scenes, covering seven key stages of McCracken's life, as it looks back at what went wrong in flashbacks in the style of Oliver Goldsmith's sentimental comedies *The Good Natured Man* and *She Stoops to Conquer*, representing the innocent optimism of the early Republican Enlightenment. This is followed by the witty repartee in the style of Wilde's *The Importance of Being Earnest* and the final bleak despair and disillusionment in Beckett's *Waiting for Godot*. Parker commented: "I found I could make each style appropriate to the situation. I could write a play set in 1798 that was speaking directly to people today. If I had written it in purely eighteenth-century style it would have seemed remote and artificial, if I had written it in complete colloquial idiom of today it would have seemed unhistorical; people dressed up in fancy clothes as if they should have been in jeans and T-shirts. The technique allowed me to march the play throughout the decades towards the present day and say to the audience, forget about historical veracity, forget about realism, I'm going to tell you a story about Republicanism and I am going to offer you a point of view on what's gone wrong with it and why it's become corrupt and why it's now serving the opposite ends to what it set out to serve." (Carty, 1985)

The scenes in the Age of Innocence are set in the Mudlers' Club in Peggy Barclay's back room where the characters, Russell, Hope and Neilson, "a bunch of wet-lipped young buckos" are plotting how to transform the world: "Ballads and toasts, toasts and ballads. Speechifying pub talk. Declarations of this, that and the other." (18) The anxious McCracken wants nothing to do with it, as he demands actions that have not been forthcoming

[130]

from the aptly named Mudlers' Club. As McCracken speaks, the ghostly figures of Russell, Hope and Neilson appear as figures of derision: "and where did it all go at the end of the evening? Pissed away into the gutter, flowing away into the night. That was the Mudlers' Club for you, better named than we knew then. The Age of Innocence that was." (18) The year is 1791, Saint Patrick's night, and the tavern keeper Peggy Barclay addresses the house in the style of Farquhar:

PEGGY: There's falsehood in fellowship, sez I. Charge our glasses, Peggy, sez they ... Old saws speak truth, and truth's a pointed thing—She that steals the honey should beware the sting! (19-20)

The evening revelry at the Mudlers' Club is filled with innuendo and insinuation as Lord Castlereagh, elected by the followers of the United Irishmen, is now considered a traitor to their cause as they seek support from President Washington in the United States, and the "Gallic constitution, as long as it remains safely in France". The early scenes in the style of Farquhar and the Age of Innocence are full of the intrigues and rumours which are circulating throughout the country about the United Irishmen. Belle, the one-time barmaid who is working for Peggy Barclay, is spying for Lord Castlereagh. He resides in Dublin and needs to be kept informed of the movements of the United Irishmen; she is, according to Russell, "his Lordship's whore ... He is even now preparing Dublin apartments for her ... And this is the cur we fought to get elected, the people's supposed champion, the apostle of reform—who now sets his whore to spy on us." (25) It is the Americans and President Washington to whom McCracken proposes his toasts in Barclay's pub and the France where, "Our Gallic brother was born 14 July, 1789." (25)

The hopes of the United Irishmen are expressed by Neilson in the Age of Innocence: "They cannot contend forever against half a million Protestant Dissenters, and three million Catholics ...

They shall unite. It is we who shall unite them. Let you weave their raiment ... whilst I print their hopes and dreams. Russell's library will educate 'em. And as for McCracken here—he shall woo them into the one bed." (26) McCracken's nightmare in the Age of Innocence augurs badly for battle to come; the four severed heads staring at him are a reminder of his men who had been hanged. "This week they've hung two of my men from Antrim ... along with two of the Ballynahinch men ... the heads have all been hacked off and impaled on spikes up on the Market House." (27) The Age of Innocence, the first of the seven ages, is all but over but there will, according to McCracken, be, "no sleep not before time. There's six more ages to straighten out. That's first. I'll be sleeping long enough soon." (27)

The Age of Idealism is cloaked in the melodrama of Dion Boucicault. Intrigue, papers, letters, and accusations abound as the local Catholic population claims to have been threatened by the Peep O'Day Boys or the Orangemen. McCracken informs the worried Catholics that everyone must abide by a simple creed: "There is strength in union, weakness in dissension. It is not the Peep O'Day Boys or the Orange Boys who threaten your livelihood and life. They themselves are your fellow prisoners in this vast cage that we call a country. It is the landlords and magistrates ... the gentlemen of rank and fortune, who deliberately foment this kind of rancour between you and your neighbours, for their own greater security. They are the cruel jailers we must unite to oppose." (30) To oppose the men of rank and fortune and to enjoy the country which is "lush and lovely", McCracken suggests they forget their differences and partake of the riches and rewards the country has to offer them, and which, if they cease to "rent each other, like caged animals, and to join with us, in the true struggle, for our mutual freedom ... You know very well there are government agents at large, working to foment these feuds between you. Every blow you strike is a self inflicted wound." (33-34)

Cleverness in the manner of Oscar Wilde is full of aphorisms and florid speech. McCracken's scene with his sister Mary Anne reveals the half-truths his middle class family have known about him. He observes: "that a man is never less true to himself than in the presence of his own family." (39) The Age of Cleverness also introduces the Belfast Harp Festival which is "famous in myth and legend ... Forging a national consciousness ... A new culture from the old ... renaissance!" (39) Atty Bunting enters to the sound of the harp and asks McCracken why he is standing outside the hall where the harp recital is taking place: "You are standing outside a musical recital talking to yourself. This is not customary in polite society. It is a position reserved for beggars and newspaper critics." Which elicits McCracken's response: "My dear Bunting. It is torment enough to have to listen to the tinkling of your harps—without the additional penance of gazing upon your harpists. Until I saw the Irish harpists, I was at a loss as to what the Irish beggars did with their cast-off clothes." (39)

Wolfe Tone enters the Belfast Harp Festival altercation where he is introduced to Bunting, who retorts, "Tone, did you say? Musical by name, but not, it would seem, by nature." To which Tone replies, "I assure you that I esteem the Irish harp above all other instruments—at any rate, up until the point when people begin to pluck at it ... You misconstrue our absence from the hall, Mr. Bunting. We [he and McCracken] are conspirators by nature. Conspirators like to listen but hate to be seen. An audience at a musical event has quite the opposite inclination. They go to be seen and never to listen." Bunting exits and Tone remarks to McCracken: "What a very disagreeable fellow, I do hope we shall see more of him. He has quite distracted me from my headache." (40-41) Tone assures McCracken that he feels confident that he can leave him to look after the northern branch of the United Irishmen. The Presbyterian north is no place for a man who enjoys consumption of liquor and certainly not the place for a southerner with a loathing of the Irish harp.

As the Age of Cleverness closes, McCracken reminds his mistress, Mary Bodle, of the high principles of his family,

THE LOST TRIBE IN THE MIRROR

particularly his grandfather, "granda Joy", who was the founder of the *Belfast News Letter* and who, at the age of ninety-three and barely alive, was carried to the polling station because he believed his vote was essential to elect John O'Neill, the great moderate reformer and United Irishman.

The Age of Dialectics, in the manner of George Bernard Shaw, opens with a scene in the derelict cottage, where McCracken and Mary await their fate at the hands of the British Dragoon Guards. This is a pivotal scene in the play as Parker introduces the Phantom Bride, who frightens off the British army, but who also lures McCracken to his fateful end. McCracken has been given false identity papers from his sister before the arrival of the Army Dragoons who are searching the slopes of Cave Hill for him. Mary-Anne McCracken arrives at the cottage, which she calls: "no fit dwelling for a patriot and a hero" to which McCracken replies: "Do you mind? You're talking about a charming rural hideaway. Convenient to town. In a much sought after area." (35) The dispute between brother and sister, over the defeat of the rising and the ensuing hunt for the members of the United Irishmen, angers McCracken. Mary-Anne says, "The coming generations will finish what you've started, they'll model themselves on your example." (36) McCracken rejects the compliment as he has failed in uniting the country to which Mary-Anne replies, "You know that won't be history's verdict." History's verdict has already been decided and is, according to McCracken, "a whore. She rides the winners." (36)

The Age of Heroism finds expression in the Hiberno-Irish grandiloquence of J.M. Synge: "The Heroic Age had arrived that day. Mad keen to fight now. Pledging ourselves for the first time to the republic of United Irishmen." (55) There is talk of freedom amongst Tone, Hope and Russell who bemoan the fact that they have always come away empty handed from their struggle with the English, however, this time they are armed and ready for battle but they acknowledge that they will never be a nation without the Protestants of the north, as Hope states: "Without the Protestants of the North, there'll never be a nation. Not without them as part of it." (57)

Compromise, the penultimate age, is reproduced in the evasive intimacies of Sean O'Casey's Dublin. McCracken realises that he must also unite the Catholic Defenders alongside him if he is to succeed in his aims of unification: "The age of compromise, the age of finally taking sides. So much for the great revolution of United Irishmen. It comes out looking like another Catholic riot." (59) Despite his cynicism McCracken accepts that he will uphold the "Catholic United States of France and Ireland and every other kingdom now in Christianity". (61)

The Age of Knowledge is written in the style of Brendan Behan and Samuel Beckett: "We finally ate of the tree of knowledge. The famous poisoned fruit. It was our last and final age. We introduced each other to it ... So they intercepted me on the road and bundled me off to Dublin. I presumed a trial would follow, but of course it never did. We were held in solitary for a while. And then herded together." (65) The Age of Knowledge dawns in prison and the play closes with McCracken's final speech and his walk to the scaffold. In the closing lines, Parker writes a threnody for Belfast, a city that is now full of "angry and implacable ghosts". (75) These words resonate as the Lambeg drum is loudly beaten: "Why would one place break your heart, more than another? A place the like of that? Brain-damaged and dangerous, continuously violating itself, a place of perpetual breakdown, incompatible voices, screeching obscenely away through the smoky dark wet. Burnt out and still burning." (75)

Heavenly Bodies

In the introduction to *Three Plays for Ireland* Parker stated they were conceived and written in consecutive order between 1983 and 1987 as a common enterprise. Shortly after he had revised *Heavenly Bodies* for this volume he died from cancer. The play has, in common with *Northern Star* and *Pentecost*, a phantom ghost appearing as the Fiddler. Dion Boucicault's father and his Mephistophelean sparring partner, Johnny Patterson, appear. Patterson's name survives precariously as a name on fading sheet music covers in 'The Garden Where the Praties Grow', 'The Stone Outside Dan Murphy's Door' and 'The Hat My Father Wore' that was altered, to become the favorite anthem of Orangeism. As *Northern Star* employed pastiche as a strategy, *Heavenly Bodies* was written as a collage. The play opens with Boucicault's death and looks back on his life and through a series of flashbacks it examines his ultimate demise with his nemesis Johnnie Patterson.

This collage-like, fictional confrontation of the two figures in *Heavenly Bodies*, from the world of showbusiness, has a realistic style and an interaction with an ostensibly surrealistic ghost. Each of the *Three Plays for Ireland* is suffused with mythical warmth, asserting Parker's belief that rational humanitarian influences exist, as a potential, in the face of complex social and political conflicts. The plays also deal, in their own individual way with the ghosts of Irish history and Parker's gifts for finding new forms of drama and metadrama to explore the complex problems of representations in Irish history.

Heavenly Bodies is set on the stage of the Madison Square Theatre, New York City, in September 1890. A class is in progress and a student, Thomas Belnap, is declaiming a speech of Faust's from *Faust and Marguerite* by Dion Boucicault. Boucicault is a teacher, three months short of seventy, who sits slumped in a bath-chair, muffled up against the cold and damp in a capacious greatcoat and muffler wearing an embroidered smoking hat on his head with two tufts of white hair protruding from the side. A second student, a tall and striking dark-haired girl, Jessie McDermot, sits to one side waiting her turn to perform with three other students. Boucicault dismisses the students, except for Jessie, to whom he confesses that he no longer remembers the name of this "vile theatre" that he believes is "Dank. The sweet sickly breathe of a dark house. I abominate a dark theatre above all other things on earth; you have learned what that means, I hope, to go dark?" (80)

Boucicault is told that Johnny Patterson, the singing clown, had been killed when an iron bar struck him as he tried to save the circus equipment from a rioting mob. Boucicault retorts: "Better still. Did he manage an exit line?" (81) The scene between Boucicault and his student is one of pathos as he realises that he has reached his own ignominious end in a 'dark' New York theatre that is like all of the other theatres where his work has been performed, it is "a monster that forgets". As he pinions Jessie to a chair he confesses, in Faustian declamation, that the theatre will demand more than her body, "It demands possession of your immortal soul ... Out there ... The jaws of the beast, stretched wide, opening up its huge dark gullet to me, oh not to bite, not any longer, it's merely yawning in my face, can you smell it, the breath? The decomposing carcass in its gut? It will swallow me now without even noticing ... " (82)

In this opening scene Boucicault is a tragic figure coming to terms with his own mistakes as he enacts scenes from his life on the eve of death. *Heavenly Bodies* is less directly political than *Northern Star* but shares with it a biographical interest in portraying an historical figure asking questions of contemporary relevance. In taking his personal revenge against society, which oppressed him socially and economically as a poor illegitimate Irishman, the question arises of whether Boucicault ignored his wider duty as an artist to his country and to his art. Boucicault was the sensation of his age in Ireland, England and the United States, but he is remembered as a perpetrator of stage-Irishry.

Dion Boucicault or Boursiquot, Dion(ysius) Lardner (1820-1890) was reared in Dublin by a family of French Huguenot descent. He was the illegitimate son of the scientist Dr. Dionysius Lardner, who became his guardian, educating him in Dublin and London where he resisted Lardner's attempts to have him trained as a railway engineer. In 1838 he became an actor with the pseudonym Lee Moreton in the English provinces. Twenty-two plays over a four-year period followed the success of his play *London Assurance*, at Covent Garden in 1841.

The fascination with Boucicault, for Parker, was his equivocal Irishness, his scepticism, his convivial pessimism, and his shameless theatricalism. Parker believed Boucicault could write a good scene, and did have some desultory concerns beyond the bank and the bedroom. There is no hint that a more principled stance in the theatre would have been more efficacious. Boucicault's personal life was torrid. After marrying a rich French widow in 1845, he went to Paris where he continued to be influenced by popular theatre. When his wife died in mysterious circumstances, he returned to London in 1848 where profligate spending soon led to bankruptcy that compelled him to return to writing for the stage.

In 1850, the actor Charles Kean took over the Princess's Theatre and made Boucicault the resident playwright. It was at the Princess's Theatre where Boucicault made his career as an actor, and where he met his future second wife, Agnes Robertson. He accompanied Robertson to the United States in 1853 where she exploited her London success and where his own acting career soon rivalled that of his wife. Attempts at managing three theatres all ended in disaster before his rise to fame with *The Colleen Bawn* in 1860. Although he had spent most of his life abroad, Boucicault saw himself as an Irishman, and despite their exploitation of stereotypical stage Irishmen, Boucicault's plays, in general, did show an awareness of Irish conditions and problems. He used his popularity to bring political concerns to wider attention, and in 1876 he wrote an open letter to the Prime Minister, Benjamin Disraeli, demanding the release of Irish political prisoners from British jails.

Whereas *Northern Star* is essentially preoccupied with the problem of political action in a society as polarised and predetermined as that of the Ulster of 1798 and 1984, the theme of *Heavenly Bodies* is the stage itself. Boucicault is seen as an ambitious theatrical vulgarian who has given a voracious public just what it wanted. Now at the moment of death he is judged and found unworthy of a place in posterity. As Patterson reminds him:

> PATTERSON: You were born a chancer and you sold your gombeen soul to the highest bidder, now—your three score years and ten are up, and your three or four entire fortunes duly made and squandered, your three or four hundred young girls come and gone ... and the account's being called in. (85)

Throughout the play Boucicault is haunted by the image of the Phantom Fiddler, who he believed to be his father. This ghostly figure haunted him throughout his life and during Boucicault's final hours becomes even more visible. His father is present, like a death's head at the feast of Boucicault's successes and examines his son's stage Irishry and melodrama on the English and American stages under the shadow of the famine.

Johnny Patterson, or Paddy the clown, who acts as Boucicault's prosecutor in his final trial, has lived as a singing clown in a travelling circus and claims that he has "kept faith with my own people, as a true clown should" and he sneers at Dion's claims to be a true artist. "So tell us, Mr. Boucicault, how did you react during the Great Irish Famine?" To which Boucicault replies: "Oh I kept London well supplied with me comedies of manners." (104)

As Boucicault looks back on his career and how he lived through his plays, which are firmly entrenched in the world of Victorian theatre, he states: "Melodrama was the raw fuel of the Age, nothing less—crude and explosive like the base culture it energised, it is literally child's play, if you've ever bothered to observe children play-acting. I was obliged to cater to child-like minds." (110) Boucicault also believed the critics had "violated, mocked and debased" his work:

> BOUCICAULT: Oh yes, the roar of the beast, that too ... I was writing comedy of manners for people who have passed beyond manners,

[139]

beyond comedy. A New Age on the rise, oh yes ... plunder and pig-ignorance, a New Dark Age of blood force, the likes of Lardner with his scientific baubles, millions enslaved by them, a raw-boned British master-race, clothing their barbarism in piety and pinstripes and fairy-princess sugar candy, what entertainment does such an age demand, do you suppose? (106)

Boucicault was a ferocious critic and a successful exponent of the forces of his age, as his wife states: "You've spent your whole career pitting yourself against the Age, fulminating against it ... when all the time the savagery of the Age was concentrated in you." (136) For Boucicault the forces of the age are concentrated in the figure of Dionysius Lardner, Boucicault's guardian who has taken the place of his rightful father and has stolen his mother. Patterson mocks Boucicault for his name and his lineage:

PATTERSON: DIONYSIUS ... LARDNER ... BOURSIQUOT, wait, wait, hang on just a minute ... I mean, what the hell class of name is that? For the son of a liquor merchant in North Dublin.
BOUCICAULT: Dionysius was a Greek god as it happens ...
PATTERSON: ... and Lardner was a Protestant goat, right?
BOUCICAULT: Dr. Lardner is neither here nor there; I am the son of Samuel Smith Boursiquot ...
PATTERSON: You're half a god and half a goat, by the sound of it.
BOUCICAULT: Samuel Smith Boursiquot, who was the descendant of a distinguished line of Huguenot immigrants ...
PATTERSON: He was a daft oul' codger, if he couldn't even make a living selling drink to the Irish. (86-87)

So obsessive is the influence of this father figure, in whose shadow Boucicault grows up, that he is unable to clear a space for his own imaginative originality, and his mother repeatedly remarks on how, like the detested Lardner, her son's ruthless ambition makes him. As well as rejecting a father, Boucicault is haunted by and in search of a father, one who is sentimentalised as an elegiac, soulful, fiddle-playing ghost of Famine Days and a symbol of disinheritance, destitution and dispossession. This is Samuel Boursiquot, now living in Athlone: "It appears he had been working in a brewery all these years in the town of Athlone, it's dead in the centre of Ireland, furthest away you can get from any coast, more or less. I expect he felt safe there. I wanted his blessing on my work." (112)

This is the father who is home, nation, the past, conscience and the knowledge of perpetual self-defeat, whose spectral authority is displaced into Boucicault's savage social criticism. Split by this dual parentage and unable to mediate between the two fathers, Boucicault's world tends to be oversimplified into a theatre of abstractions, or types which must behave with a decorum of extremes and melodrama. The 'raw-boned' theatre manager, who is British and dressed in pinstripes, encourages Boucicault: "Melodrama, Dion. The people want melodrama ... The French, Dion, look at the French. Boulevards ahead of us, in the melodrama stakes. Why not pop over to Paris and see what you can gather up?" (106)

Melodrama was the backbone of the Covent Garden Theatre whose manager, Charles Matthews, and his wife, Madame Vestris, provided popular theatre with inferior scripts. They had suggested to Boucicault that he change the name of his first script *Out of Town* to *London Assurance*: "Dion, my darling, this title *Out of Town*—it's too homespun for such a momentous debut, it makes the wrong emphasis, the title should proclaim your arrival in our midst, your triumph over wild and primitive origins, it should hoist your banner, you are assured of a great success in the premier theatre of England—what do you say to *London Assurance*?" (101)

Boucicault was undoubtedly a pawn for the theatre management as he churned out scores of plays for the London stage. According to his sparring partner Johnny Patterson, he was a walking testimonial to those values that made the Victorian age a golden one with greed, ruthlessness, pious self-righteousness and hypocrisy. Johnny Patterson serves as the antagonist and the catalyst in the play and in terms of the play's strenuous dialectic, it is a fractured image. There are Boucicault's assertions of artistic sensibility and civilized mind and there is Johnny's insistence that Boucicault was as much a clown as he was a "chancer" who had signed away his soul long ago to showbusiness. Patterson reminds him that he is not the legitimate heir to the English stage, following Richard Brinsley Sheridan and Oliver Goldsmith: "Irishmen all, but conquerors of the English stage—and taking over the torch now, Dionysius Lardner Boucicault! Quote—'Mr. Boucicault's *London Assurance* is the legitimate heir of *The Recruiting Officer*, *She Stoops to Conquer*, *The School for Scandal* ... in brief, he is the authentic comedy genius of the Age' ... that was what you were petrified they wouldn't say, am I right?" (102)

> BOUCICAULT: I walked back into the theatre; it was ringing with laughter and cheers. I rushed in, the place was jammed, I saw the final scene, there was a cataclysm of joy, I was manhandled on to the stage to receive the roar of the beast, the curtain descended for the final time, I was engulfed in rapture!
>
> PATTERSON: Yeah, I know the feeling.
>
> BOUCICAULT: You? You have no idea what I'm talking about, don't try to compare the circus ring with the legitimate stage!
>
> PATTERSON: Fine word. Legitimate.
>
> BOUCICAULT: I was acclaimed as the great rising dramatic poet of the Age!
>
> PATTERSON: Now, gods, stand up for bastards. (102)

After the success of *London Assurance* when he was twenty-years old, Boucicault was the 'hired clerk' of the theatre, forced into writing, and in many cases, plagiarising French farces. Court proceedings were initiated against him accusing him of being 'a bare-faced plagiarist' and he retorted by making a virtue out of the crime he has committed: "Show me a single place where I have despoiled genius, other than to make the beast worship it." He longed to be a part of the illustrious Irish tradition of Farquhar, Congreve and Sheridan.

Johnny Patterson is a decisive presence in the play with his balladeering and attacks on Boucicault. He is 'Paddy the Clown' who has lived as a singing clown in a travelling circus and claims that he has "kept faith with my own people as a true clown should". (104) Johnny's claim to fame is as a writer of popular songs, 'The Stone Outside Dan Murphy's Door' a record of which, according to Parker, was the most cherished offering on his grandfather Jimmy Lynas's old wind-up gramophone. In his obituary, he is called: "Patterson the Irish Singing clown who was a devout patriot of his native Ireland, who nevertheless had come to believe that the one hope for that troubled isle lay in a commingling of the Orange and the Green ... " (81) Boucicault replies: "You have to be a real clown to believe that." (81) At the end of Act 1 Patterson sings 'The Garden Where the Praties Grow' when he appears as the masked Phantom Fiddler, who with "a bloodcurdling laugh", whips off his hat to reveal himself.

Patterson is scathing of Boucicault: "You flattered the daylights out of them, with your silver-tongued, charming peasant rascals and all their winning, wheedling and conniving ways ... your colonial soul discovered its strength in fraudulence and deceit ... you were in the conjuring business, you conjured up a never-never emerald island, fake heroics and mettlesome beauties and villains made of pasteboard, outwitted through eternity by the bogus grinning peasant rogue as only you could play him—with blather and codology and gaslight moonshine." (134)

Doubts over Boucicault's artistic sensibility and his lack of social conscience in his plays is questioned as half of his countrymen starved to death, or were forced into exile while he wrote about *Heavenly Bodies*, Irish heiresses and London Assurance. Boucicault insisted that he did confront the major issues of the day including slavery in *The Indian Mutiny* and *The Octoroon*. "I knew in my bones the meaning of enslavement and dispossession, I carried the stigmata of a supposed child of nature,

[143]

of an artist amongst the barbarians, of a licensed song and dance man for the British Empire, that was why I gambled everything on that play! Every cent I'd earned had been spent on the Winter Garden Theatre, I'd only opened it two months previously, if *The Octoroon* had failed I would have gone under ... " (121) This social concern was only for profit, according to Patterson, and the plays were the flattering conceit of a colonial soul dealing in sentimental fraudulence. On his own account, the grounds of Boucicault's opposition to enslavement are shifting and contradictory; one moment he opposes it in terms of moral principle and the next in the much less elevated terms of self-interest.

This lack of self mastery extends into his personal life, that he identifies with his mother, and fills him with Hamlet-like disgust: "You made yourself a slave, I won't live like that, mother—I am going to master my own fate, however hard they ensnare and cage me." (127) Boucicault never manages to master his own fate and personal dignity is as elusive as artistic or political integrity. He proclaims his refusal to be condemned to live as a farce just at the point when, in a scene from his play, *The Jilt*, we see him disappear into Colonel Gibbon's bedroom to avoid discovery by the irate George Jordan, with whose wife he has been having one of his clandestine affairs. When Boucicault disowns Agnes to live with Louise Thorndyke (she was twenty-one, Boucicault, sixty-five), Johnny tells him that he has reduced his wife to a harlot in the eyes of society and seen his children illegitimised and dispossessed. Patterson tells him these are "the very grievances you've been whingeing about all morning" and ironically these "grievances" also represent the values of a narrow, conventionalised society against which Boucicault is in revolt.

Boucicault had written over two hundred plays during a thirty-year period and in his old age liked to quote and perform scenes from his work, often revealing his inability to discern between reality and the theatre. Parker inserts scenes from several of Boucicault's canon of works in *Heavenly Bodies*: "May I now humbly offer you in return a few lines from a part I composed many years ago for Mr. Charles Kean, later to comprise one of the greatest triumphs of my dear good friend Mr. Irvine ... from Act Four of my *Louis XI*." (83) The older actors demanded an exit line which Boucicault had been loath to give them, and he himself is now looking for a climactic line for the end of his own life but cannot resolve his own exit: "They were accustomed to exit lines, you see, without them they felt simply stranded on the stage. They used to say to me: dear boy, can't you possibly offer me a few words to take me off, you've left me high and dry ... " (141) The only home Boucicault has is the theatre, the realm of perpetual play.

The farcical wake scene from *The Shaughraun* at the end of *Heavenly Bodies* redeems Boucicault and allows the audience to forgive him his philandering and political and artistic compromises. The audience knows that Conn is actually alive but his mother and neighbours take him for dead: "He was brave! He was brave! He had the heart of a lion and the legs of a fox ... His voice was softer than the cuckoo of an evening, and sweeter than the blackbird after a summer shower. Ye colleens, ye will never hear the voice of Conn again!" to which Conn replies, "It's a mighty pleasant thing to die like this, once in a way, and hear all the good things said about ye after ye're dead and gone, when they can do you no good." (142-43)

The challenge for Parker, in his apocalyptic project *Three Plays for Ireland*, was to find the possibility of hope and transcendence. This challenge was, not merely to reflect the ideological forces of the age, but also, to reach beyond them and to see the truth, which that ideology conceals. The final play in the trilogy, *Pentecost* (1987), gave him the distance he needed to write dispassionately and with vision for a future in which the ghosts of the past fifteen years could finally be laid to rest.

Pentecost

Pentecost opened on 23 September 1987 in the Guildhall in

Londonderry. It was directed by Patrick Mason and produced and toured by the Field Day Theatre Company. Parker was exploring ways to transcend the self-destructive myths, that have shaped the political and social life in Northern Ireland. *Pentecost* begins during the Ulster Workers' Strike in 1974 and contains a fascinating range of viewpoints on the civil unrest that surrounded the events of that year. The only hope of redemption, from Parker's perspective and to end the civil conflict, rested on individual humanity. Though the characters in *Pentecost* are from both Catholic and Protestant backgrounds, the territory of the play is literally and imaginatively Protestant; militant Protestantism with the Bible in one hand and the pickaxe handle in the other. *Pentecost* is a problem play with a rhetorical ending in which Parker attempted to point a way forward for the fractured Northern Irish society. The play completed his trilogy, or triptych, of history plays. Parker preferred 'triptych' saying that 'trilogy' is too strong for their relationship. (Parker, 1989)

In his introduction to the plays, he described them as "three self-contained groups of figures from the eighteenth, nineteenth and twentieth centuries, hinged together in a continuing comedy of terrors". (9) Parker was a whimsical and elegiac writer and in *Pentecost*, one of his 'densest' plays, his writing is wryly despairing and poetically positive, creating an atmosphere that shows the fall of man and his hoped-for redemption.

In *Three Plays for Ireland* Parker's apocalyptic project was to try to find reconciliation and transcendence in the abyss of the social disorder in Northern Ireland. A closer examination of the 1974 conflict is necessary to understand the personal conflicts between Marion, Lenny, Ruth, Peter and the ghost of Lily Mathews. The play is Parker's most intimate and the most daring as he articulates hope for a spiritual regeneration through personal grace.

The five years preceding the strike of 1974 had left 1,000 dead (620 in Belfast alone) and 25,000 homes destroyed. Before the collapse of the Sunningdale Agreement in 1974, there had been eleven murders and thirteen bombs, and the atmosphere in Northern Ireland was tense. In the first four years of the Troubles, somewhere between 30,000 and 60,000 people in the greater Belfast area were driven to leave their homes. At that time it was possibly the largest enforced movement of population in Europe since the Second World War.

The conflict by 1974 had been raging for almost five years as IRA bombs continued to demolish Belfast while the citizens of the city were also dying at the hands of terrorists. The background to the events of 1974 began in March 1973 when a White Paper, published by the Heath Government in London, proposed a 78-member assembly in Northern Ireland to be elected by proportional representation and accompanied by a Council of Ireland. On 28 June, elections to the Northern Ireland Assembly were held. The Social and Democratic Labour Party (SDLP) won 19 seats; Unionists (faithful to party leader Brian Faulkner) 23 seats; Unionists opposed to the White Paper 10 seats, the Paisley-Craig coalition (hardline loyalist) 15 seats and the Alliance Party 8 seats.

In November 1974 the coalition of Faulkner's unionists, the SDLP and the Alliance Party took office with Faulkner as the Chief Executive and Gerry Fitt (SDLP) as his deputy. The Sunningdale Conference on 6 December convened to finalise agreement on the Council of Ireland's function and composition. After three days, the Republic's Taoiseach (Prime Minister) Liam Cosgrave and Brian Faulkner's executive reached an agreement.

The beginning of the New Year in 1974 did not augur well for the new executive when Faulkner resigned as leader of the Unionist Party because of his party's opposition to the Sunningdale Agreement, but he remained the chief executive of the Northern Ireland Assembly. On 28 February the British election produced a new Labour government defeating Ted Heath's Conservative Party. The United Ulster Unionist Council, the grand loyalist coalition, opposed to Sunningdale

[147]

and power sharing, won eleven out of the twelve Northern Ireland seats. Harold Wilson, the newly elected British Prime Minister, warned loyalists there could be no turning back on the Sunningdale Agreement.

On 14 May the Assembly voted on a proposal to renounce the Sunningdale Agreement; the Ulster Unionist Council was defeated by 44 votes to 28. An all-out strike was called immediately by the Ulster Workers' Council that began on 15 May. During the following days the electricity workers joined the strike, forcing essential services to collapse. On 25 May, Harold Wilson broadcast his infamous 'spongers' speech to the nation, in which he announced that the British army would be sent to Northern Ireland. On 28 May Faulkner resigned and Wilson suspended the Northern Ireland Assembly. It was Sunday, 2 June, *Pentecost* Sunday.

It would be necessary to go back to the United Irishmen in 1798 to find a period when a part of the population of the United Kingdom became ungovernable. The Protestant Workers established a self-elected government in Northern Ireland, supported by a well-armed private army and extremist politicians who helped to break up the civilized life of the country. The population during the two-week strike was deprived of life's basic amenities. The British army was paralysed by the extent of the strike and was unable, and unwilling, to maintain essential services. British soldiers became gravediggers and at one point during the strike believed they would be preparing for food riots in the streets of Northern Ireland as British Government plans included outbreaks of disease in Ulster cities. Only the capitulation of the Assembly, the democratically elected body, would bring the strike to an end. The strikers established a *de facto* provisional government with the Loyalist paramilitary organisations directing essential services.

Religious leaders were implicated in the paralysis of Northern Ireland as they believed that theirs was a just struggle in the eyes of God, and a righteous struggle against the attempts of the

British Government to exercise its will on the Protestant majority. Billy Kelly, one of the Ulster Workers' Council leaders, and a member of the Pentecostal church, listed biblical references that he believed were apposite to the strike from both the Old and New Testaments.

The mood in the nationalist community was tense, but indifferent. The Protestant paramilitaries had succeeded in shutting down Northern Ireland, something the Republican movement had been unable to achieve in its five-year armed struggle. Many Republican families travelled to the south of Ireland, fearing that Republican estates would go undefended if the Protestant militias attacked them. This feeling of mutual struggle was shared by both Protestant and Catholic as they were trying to live without essential services.

Harold Wilson's speech to the nation opens Act 2 of *Pentecost*. Over the theatre PA the audience hears the opening of the broadcast that continues while Ruth enters the kitchen from the hallway. She has a lighted candle in one hand and a transistor radio in the other. The sound of the broadcast from her radio overlaps with, and soon takes over from, the theatre PA:

> The people on this side of the water—British parents—have seen their sons vilified and spat upon and murdered. British taxpayers have seen the taxes they have poured out, almost without regard to cost—over three hundred million pounds a year, this year with the cost of the Army operation on top of that—going into Northern Ireland. They see property destroyed by evil violence and are asked to pick up the bill for rebuilding it. Yet people who benefit from all this now viciously defy Westminster, purporting to act as though they were an elected government; people who spend their lives sponging on Westminster and British democracy and then systematically assault democratic methods. Who do these people think they are? (*Pentecost*, 182-83)

The Protestant and British residents of Northern Ireland had been particularly offended by Wilson's speech as the Ulster

[149]

Protestants had been proud of their triumph over Nationalism embodied in the Stormont Parliament. Stormont opened in 1932 in a building that fulfilled James Craig's wish for the dignity and permanence of the Ulster Parliament. The imposing building with its classical style and lavish interiors dwarfed, in scale and grandeur, the town house of the Duke of Leinster that serves as the Irish Parliament.

Act 1 of *Pentecost* opens on a night in February and Act 2 focuses on the two weeks of the strike between May 19 and June 2. Four ordinary people and the ghost of Lily Mathews are gathered together in the living room of a Belfast home in the east of the city. In this room they are trying to solve their relationships with each other against the background of the Ulster Workers' strike. Parker shares O'Casey's concerns with characters trapped by the politico-religious vendettas of Ireland and he also follows O'Casey in the contrast he draws between the loquaciously irresponsible male and the agonised, but strong woman, who struggles to articulate the author's message. *Pentecost* conveys the frightened feeling of life in Belfast where the characters joke about the absurdity of the situation as they try to remove themselves from the festering bigotry.

Pentecost is a naturalistic play and takes place in a living room. Coming from outside are the sounds and messages of a determining and frustrating world, while inside the house the vigorously naturalistic dialogue, between four people, reflects the sickness of the outside world. As Parker stated in the introduction to *Three Plays for Ireland*: "Plays and ghosts have a lot in common", and in *Pentecost* the cycle of retribution is finally laid to rest in the ghost of Lily Mathews. The loss of a future is a prominent motif in the play as plot revelations about an abandoned baby, three miscarriages, a cot death, and an impotent husband make emphatically clear. The reverberations of two broken marriages pervade the play along with a bitter reliving of the past that prevents the characters from moving forward. To escape from possession from a vengeful past, the characters must undergo a catharsis, if any future is to be imagined.

A more and more evangelical tone builds towards the image of being 'born again', using the language of the Bible with an intensity and fervour that belongs only to the Protestant tradition. Passages from the Bible are quoted in *Pentecost* as emotional touchstones, with themes that are intensely puritan. Throughout the play the puritan division between the mind and the body is juxtaposed, between spirituality on the one hand, and sexuality on the other.

People have gathered in the house of Lily Mathews to escape the forces that are tearing the city apart. Marian is a woman struggling for her own liberation which, at the end, she partially achieves. The play is not an assessment of Marian alone, but rather of each of the group who, collectively, are misfits seeking their own redemption. The ghost of Lily Mathews hovers about the house, which lies in the no-man's-land between the warring factions. As an embittered Protestant, she resents seeing 'Popeheads' in her house who are 'smelling of the mass'. Lenny is a former lawyer, now an unemployed trombone player, and his friend Peter, a Birmingham surveyor scornful of Northern Ireland's self-absorbed littleness. Peter, the son of a Methodist minister, has returned for a brief visit from his exile in England where he has become well travelled and cosmopolitan. Like Julian in *Spokesong*, he is also the returned cynic and the predatory opportunist trying to escape his Northern Irish background.

Lenny and Peter recall their exploits during student days in Belfast when they might have stopped what Parker called Ulster's continuing "comedy of terrors". They had planned to add the hallucinatory drug LSD into Belfast's water supply and hoped to 'space-out' the entire population on a peace-and-love trip. The plan did not materialise, as they were unaware that the Ulster Volunteer Force had blown up the Silent Valley Reservoir and Belfast was already without water. They had hoped to see the "population, comprehensively, with one simple transcendental gesture, that would be it, the doors of perception flung wide, wholesale mind-shift, no more bigotry and hatred, a city full of spaced-out contemplatives like the three of us". (201) Parker dispenses with the perspective of history to find a telling detachment in *Pentecost*, and the humour in his work can surface so that he can cloak his agonised concern over the lunacies of sectarian fanaticism in such whimsicalities.

Marian, Lenny's estranged wife, is a former antiques dealer. Ruth, her friend, is escaping to the house from her own estranged, psychopathic husband. Both women are haunted by a past that is made tangible through Lily Mathews who, with her stern, unyielding Protestant attitudes, disapproves of the Catholic Marian. Marian's is the one voice that is raised above the impotent confusion in Lily Mathews' house as she acts to force confrontation with the past.

Lily haunts Marian as she has discovered her reading her diaries and searching among her other belongings that embody the Protestant history in twentieth-century Belfast. Lily Mathews' life has been one of suffering, guilt and denial and her insistence that through her personal trials, she "never surrendered, not one inch", makes her an incarnation of the embattled mentality of her entire community. There is an intimate bonding between Marian and Lily, despite Lily's vitriol, as Marian forces Lily to acknowledge her past and to accept what has happened and to move on.

Marian is obsessed with Lily Mathews' home, and is determined to keep it unchanged, in every detail, as a monument to the past, where nothing has altered since it was built:

MARIAN: Lily Mathews lived here. 1900 to 1974. This house was her whole life. She never threw anything away. I've started cataloguing it all. Every last thimble and shirt stud, every grocery bill and cigarette card and rationing coupon, every document of her and Alfie's life together. (177)

Marian wants to sell the house to the National Trust because it is quite un-modernised and unspoiled; the furnishings and ornaments have been unchanged for decades with nothing newer than a 1953 coronation mug. Marian is contemptuous of the Belfast bourgeoisie:

> MARIAN: In my case the embattled bourgeoisie of Belfast was one long procession of avaricious gobshites—hell-bent on overloading their lounge cabinets and their display units with any bauble or knick-knack, so long as it looked like it cost more than it did, so long as it was showy enough to advertise their grandeur, and their fashionable taste and stylishness, not to mention their absolutely bottomless vulgarity, it was bad enough before the shooting-match started, it's grotesque at this point. (151)

Parker reveals a fascinating range of viewpoints in *Pentecost* on the problems of Northern Ireland that are seen festering through the generations. He introduces a metaphor of a land unfit for babies. Lily's husband, Alfie, had been unemployed for two years at the height of the depression, during which time they took a lodger, Alan Ferris. While her husband was in England, Lily had Ferris' child that she abandoned after birth, on the steps of the Baptist church:

> MARIAN: You left him lying on the porch of a Baptist Church.
> LILY: A well-off congregation, it was for the best ... moneyed people ... some pair of them would take him in, adopt him as their own, what did you want me to do ...
> MARIAN: He would have had his best chance right here, being reared by you and Alfie ...
> LILY: Alfie was impotent, wasn't he. A souvenir of Passchendaele maybe. Scarcely the first nor the last to come back from the dead in that condition. (195-196)

Marian and Lily look for meaning in existence but despite the bitterness and hopelessness that prevails, they seem bound by

[153]

what Parker once described as the two communities' "compact of mutual impotence and sterility" and also by their own personal experiences of separation, loss and childlessness. Lily's bouts of bitter self-righteousness and her poignant reflections during her childless marriage are also reflected in the lives of Marian and Ruth. Marian refers to the house as "a childless house" and calls it "barren" but she believes she feels so at home there because her child, Christopher, died in infancy and Ruth has had three miscarriages. The three women attempt to create a future in a hellish situation, or as Peter wryly states: "The church invented hell. They've just used this town to show us what they mean." (206)

Parker evangelises to end the "sacrilege on life", for a vigilant and creative use of the past to transcend the self-destructive myths and stereotypes that have imprisoned the population of Northern Ireland. *Pentecost* is "a play in which a home acquires a national symbolism. As in George Bernard Shaw's fantasia *Heartbreak House* there is more conversation than plot, but there is a crucial difference between Parker's play and Shaw's. Where Shaw's English drifters welcome the Zeppelins that will destroy their meaningless existence, Parker's Marian enters a heartfelt and moving plea for spiritual regeneration. In the final moments of the play there are too many attempts to see Marian and her trio of lodgers as an archetypal Irish or Holy family. It is, however, an extraordinary play in how much of Belfast Stewart Parker manages to put on the stage in the politics, religion and the tension between residents and exiles. The idea of a city, and country, haunted by its past and forever fuelled by a righteous anger, is what makes the play so moving, as it is Stewart Parker's burning conviction that recrimination is not enough. (Billington, 1989)

Pentecost demonstrates the difficulties and dangers Parker faces in dramatising his unique vision. Its ending is clumsily forced and impatient, although passionate surges are undeniable: "There are a series of anecdotal epiphanies in which the characters talk past each other, but like Beckett's characters, they urge each other to keep talking. What makes Stewart Parker such an exciting dramatist is his dynamic outlook in the depth and completeness of his interrogation of the lives and conditions of his characters, Catholic and Protestant, without fear and compromise, so that between author and audience common recognition emerges, a supervening bond above and beyond ideas." (Andrews, July-September 1989)

Pentecost is a play by a man whose vision, understanding and humour have sculpted a challenging work for the theatre and is arguably, Parker's greatest achievement. As a playwright he was reaching the height of his career. However wry and caustic the dialogue between the characters is, however desperate and angry they are, they have all achieved a form of exorcism by the end of the play from which grow varying degrees of optimism. Each character has in the final act a lyrical speech or a Pentecostal incantation in which a vengeful past is rejected and faith in a future is expressed. Marian symbolically decides to renovate rather than preserve the house and appeals to reject recrimination and to accept a real faith in the future:

> MARIAN: Personally, I want to live now. I want this house to live. We have committed sacrilege enough on life, in this place, in these times. We don't just owe it to ourselves, we owe it to our dead too ... our innocent dead. They're not our masters, they're only our creditors, for the life they never knew. We owe them at least that— the fullest life for which they could have ever hoped, we carry those ghosts within us, to betray those hopes is the real sin against the Christ, and I for one cannot commit it one day longer. (208)

John Hume, the SDLP politician, commented after seeing *Pentecost* in Derry that it was an important work for Ireland as it shared such humanity and compassion.

"Stewart Parker's plays bear testimony to an acute intelligence and brilliant imagination which probed the secrets and stories of diverse tribes inhabiting Ireland. He saw that same country with strange eyes, and appropriately so, for Ireland revealed to Stewart Parker that strange capacity to wound and separate and bind and heal its people, avoiding at all cost to agree the common name of Irish with all the terrors that name implies. With his Masters thesis in poetic drama Stewart Parker began work on a theatrical form which is the inheritance of every Irish playwright and he realised that inheritance by foregrounding contemporary music through his dramatic language." (McGuinness, 1989)

Fanaticism was for Parker the most dangerous thing in life, and even though his plays rarely moved out of Ireland, they continued to release his creative energy and, despite the stasis of the Northern Ireland troubles, it was for him a creative wellspring. As Seamus Heaney has written, Parker possessed: "Folk wisdom and a natural sense of Northern Downbeat." Heaney regarded him as a writer with an edge of risk in his work, a chance deliberately taken in the treatment: "And this was all of a piece with his fine inclination to keep displacing himself from every easy opinion and predictable move ... Stewart Parker was beloved for his intrinsic personal qualities. His presence rang true ... He was one of those you went towards with gratitude and without premeditation, and came away from with a renewed trust in the very possibility in trust itself ... He was authentic, somebody you could call, without embarrassment, a good man. And he was also a necessary man, not least in the way he manifested style, tolerance, mobility and stamina ... He stood for that victory over the negative aspects of Ulster intolerance which everybody wants to believe is possible." (Heaney, 1988) While at Queen's University Parker contracted bone cancer and had his leg amputated. This wound played its part in his writing, not in self-pity or cynicism, but in a joyous determination to celebrate life in all of its struggle, and defeats, and the ability to transcend suffering.

Parker believed that a playwright should be a truth-teller and a sceptic in a credulous world and this he translated into his own writing with new forms of inclusiveness that transformed drama about Northern Ireland. In doing so, he found a means of representing universal truths that did not centre on the violence in Northern Ireland and often touched upon it obliquely. His background as a Northern Irish Protestant informs his work, but it is also a testimony in his belief to stay clear of the 'traps and snares' to which the playwright from Northern Ireland could be prone. Plays set on the streets of Belfast could reflect certain aspects of life there but they would fail to reflect adequately upon them.

Irish history is like the theatre, a recurring history as: "Ancestral voices ... and the ghosts of your own time and birthplace wrestle and dance, in any play you choose to write— but most obviously when it is a history play." (Parker, 1989) Gary Mitchell's play *Tearing the Loom* shares, with Parker's *Northern Star*, the events of 1798. Whereas Parker had an academic training, inhabiting the world as a metropolitan intellectual whose plays require us to maintain a cool, Brechtian distance, Gary Mitchell, although also a member of the 'lost tribe', comes from a very different background. His work is much more akin to the naturalism of Sam Thompson and his deliberately provocative realism. Mitchell plays are brutal family plays; he is a proletarian playwright who takes the audience into the underworld of the mob as he unfolds life among the lowly.

The 'traps and snares' that face the Ulster playwright, in writing about Northern Ireland are, according to Stewart Parker, dangerous ground for the theatre. Parker's creative distancing is an anathema to Gary Mitchell who subjects his audience to brutal confrontations between the paramilitary organisations and the families whose lives are governed by them. The challenges facing the Protestant population changed dramatically during the 1990s as the breakup of the old order began and new identities were being forged within the Protestant community. Stewart Parker's imaginative territory is transformed in Mitchell's work that is informed by an uneasy peace in Ulster in which internal conflict, within the sectarian divide, is omnipresent and presents the conflict in stark brutal images.

[157]

CHAPTER FIVE

Gary Mitchell
Refracting the Mirror

Gary Mitchell is one of a growing number of Northern Irish playwrights responsible for injecting a new spirit into Irish theatre. His imaginative landscape is focused on a claustrophobic Northern Irish community where every action is questioned and every word carefully weighed, in a sad and often brutal world. In 1991, three years after Stewart Parker's death, Mitchell began his writing career in the midst of Protestant militancy in a suburban housing estate north of Belfast.

Mitchell's work over the past fifteen years includes ten scripts for film and television: *Falling* (2005) Channel Four; *Sexton* (2004) BBC Northern Ireland; *Energy* (2003/4) FilmFour; *Feud* (2003/4) BBC Northern Ireland; *The Force of Change* (2003/4) BBC Northern Ireland; *Suffering* (2003) BBC Northern Ireland; *As the Beast Sleeps* (2001/2) BBC 2, screened at film festivals in Edinburgh, New York, London, Montreal, Belfast, Wales, Gothenburg, Boston; awarded Third Place, Prix Europa (2002); winner, Belfast Arts Award for Television (2002); *Once Upon a Time in Belfast* (2000/1) DNA Films; *An Officer from France* (1998) RTE; *Red White and Blue* (1998) BBC1. For radio: *As the Beast Sleeps* (2001) Radio 4; *Drumcree* (1996) BBC4, shortlisted for Sony Award; *Poison Hearts* (1995) BBC4; *Stranded* (1995) BBC 3;

Independent Voice (1995) BBC4, winner of the Stewart Parker Award, BBC Radio Drama (1994); *The World, the Flesh and the Devil* (1991) BBC4, Award winner, Young Playwrights Festival. Mitchell's plays for the theatre include: *State of Failure* (2006); *Remnants* (2006); *Something to Believe In* (2005); *Deceptive Imperfections* (2003); *Splinters* (2003); *Loyal Women* (2003); *Marching On* (2001); *The Force of Change* (2000), winner, *Evening Standard* Charles Wintor Award for Most Promising Playwright, joint winner of the George Devine Award, nominated for a South Bank Show Award; *Convictions: 'Holding Cell'* (2000), winner ESB *Irish Times* Best Production Award; *Energy* (1999); *Trust* (1999) Winner of Pearson Best Play of the Year Award; *As the Beast Sleeps* (1998); *Tearing the Loom* (1998); *In a Little World of Our Own* (1997), winner of Irish Theatre's Best New Play award, Winner of Belfast Arts Drama Award; *Sinking* (1997), winner of Belfast Drama Award; *That Driving Ambition, Alternative Future, Exodus, Suspicious Minds, Independent Voice* (1995).

There has been a strong demand for Protestants to examine their culture in Northern Ireland as the years of violence ended with a peace accord in 1995. Mitchell's own personal success suggests the presence of an interest in Protestantism as a community and an identity. He states: "I think that the kind of scripts and plays that were available for many years were very poor. I think that's one reason why we haven't done so well. Recently many fine writers have come out of the woodwork. As far as Northern Ireland is concerned, there is a sort of grievance that writers tend to be nationalist or Catholic ... There are a lot of Protestant writers appearing here and there because Protestantism is changing." (Mooney, 1997)

Mitchell left Rathcoole Secondary School when he was sixteen and joined Northern Ireland's ranks of unemployed. He was, as he readily admits, a perfect candidate for the paramilitary organisation, the UDA, in north Belfast, which Mitchell's family supported until it was declared illegal in 1992. Rathcoole was a desolate claustrophobic environment in which he had to learn to survive: "I passed the 11-plus but my parents couldn't afford to send me to a proper school so I went to a terrible one ... what I learnt I learnt in the playground. How to take punches and kicks and get up and walk away, to use my brain to talk my way out of difficult situations ... It is a murky area of my life. I was like any other young man going down a hard road and doing terrible things. I have remorse but I also feel I was led ... I was psychologically damaged before I was born. I thought I had a predetermined place, to man the barricades and defend our country." (Boland, 1997)

During his formative years, Mitchell admits to never thinking about the Irish Republic or what it meant to be Irish: "I was just a Protestant person who lived in a Protestant place that was totally British, in a way my education began at Sunday School. It was there I was introduced to God and Jesus Christ as my own personal saviour. And basically, I found out that the Pope was the anti-Christ, that Roman Catholics were the enemy and we, the Protestants, were in fact the chosen people. In 1974, when I was still a young boy, during the Workers' Strike, barricades went up around the Protestant areas all over the country. I suddenly had this image that this is our life—that we've erected this wall around ourselves because there is something out there that's trying to harm us. And it's like a scar, that no matter how intellectual you become, no matter how distanced you feel, you'll never really heal, that outside this area you are never really safe." (*Ibid*, 1997)

Mitchell managed to stay out of the paramilitary organisation and found an 'unchallenging' job as a civil servant: "It was a hideous reward ... I felt I was losing my dignity, doing monkey work among the robots ... I felt it was degrading." (*Ibid*) Fighting the conviction that, as a working-class man, he was not allowed to become a writer, he wrote a play that began through improvisation with the Belfast Youth Theatre, under the direction of Peter Quigley, from whom he borrowed an Olivetti typewriter. He entered his first scripted play, *The World, the Flesh and the Devil* (1991) for a radio competition. He won the competition, and with encouragement from director Pam Brighton he began his career as a playwright.

In writing from a Protestant perspective, Gary Mitchell shares with Thompson and Parker close observations of the working-class Protestant world of Belfast. The political climate during the 1990s in Northern Ireland had changed and a new landscape had evolved that Thompson and Parker would not have recognised. More than thirty years earlier, Thompson and his players had had to form their own company to stage *Over the Bridge*, as the Group Theatre's board of directors had rejected it, and Parker found it almost impossible to have his work premiered in Belfast. Mitchell faced similar rejections as he premiered his 1997 play *In a Little World of Our Own* at the Peacock auditorium of the Abbey Theatre in Dublin and not the Lyric Theatre in Belfast. The play received three awards and was voted Best New Play at the Irish Theatre Awards in 1997.

Mitchell is a lone voice in his philosophy and his political preoccupation with his Rathcoole community. His belief that Protestantism has been misrepresented by the media, theatre, and film-makers and by Protestants themselves, is central to his work: "There is a deep mistrust of the media and a paranoia that only one side of the story is ever told. Admittedly, they have made mistakes by not coming forward with their own stories and versions of events, for fear of being misrepresented ... The other problem is that Protestantism is deeply divided internally, at the moment, and the voices we do hear need to be replaced from within. It's a hard road, but people are beginning to walk it." (Coyle, 1997)

Middle-class Unionists, who were deeply suspicious of anything that did not fit into their own narrow view of the world, rejected Thompson's play *Over the Bridge*. The Unionists did not initiate the rejection of Mitchell's work but they reflected what has been a common trait in Ulster theatre, the great gift of not recognising indigenous talent. The Lyric Theatre did encourage Mitchell to finish *Dividing Force*: "The Lyric had an open door policy and invited anyone to come in with ideas. What I took to them was only an idea, through dialogue, and although they didn't want to do anything with it, they did encourage me to go on and finish the play." (Moore, 1997) When the play was completed, Mitchell found initial interest with the Tinderbox Theatre Company in Belfast: "They had the play for eighteen months ... but during that time turned it down in favour of other productions. When they were about to reject it a third time I took it back." (*Ibid*)

The success of the Dublin and Belfast productions of Mitchell's plays led to his appointment as writer-in-residence at the Royal National Theatre in London under the Pearson Television Theatre Writers' Scheme, a twelve-month appointment committing him to write one new play for the theatre. When he began writing, Mitchell stated that his horizons stretched as far as the Lyric Theatre in Belfast. Many of his works were later performed in London theatres.

A peaceful solution for Northern Ireland has become a tangible reality since the Peace Agreement of 1995 that initiated a shift in the previous decades' political and violent impasse. The echo of Stewart Parker's plea in *Pentecost* for reconciliation is reiterated in Mitchell's work. The possibility of Catholic and Protestant living peacefully, side by side, is perhaps more tangible today than it was in 1987 when *Pentecost* was written. And yet, despite all the peace initiatives, the ghettoisation of Belfast, between Protestant and Catholic, is more pronounced in 2009 than during the previous thirty years.

Mitchell's work examines a house in disorder in the Rathcoole estate, where paramilitary forces have dictated their own laws during years of sectarian violence. Several of his plays examine life in the Protestant ghetto as he attempts to point a way forward for an understanding, and acceptance, of Protestant culture in Northern Ireland. As he writes: "because I think it's important that the world just doesn't see one side of Northern

Ireland. We have been complaining for years about how we are misunderstood and misrepresented in the world, by 'we' I'm talking about the Northern Protestants in general. Continually, our criticism has been outward, they don't understand us, and they write bad things about us. It's always they. And I've always said, well what are we going to do about it?" (Fricker, 1998)

The Protestant community in Rathcoole had done a very poor job of presenting its case to the world. Mitchell claims that the beliefs and cultural values of the Ulster Protestant are misunderstood, misrepresented and considered narrow-minded and intolerant.

Mitchell explores the extent to which history can often ignore the psychological roots of conflict in Northern Ireland. He recalls the eerie separation of Protestants and Catholics that fed his childhood paranoia: "It starts to draw you back into yourself ... you don't want to leave your house, you don't want to leave your street, because the further away from home you get, there are people who hate you with every thread of their being, and they live their lives just waiting, stalking the areas, waiting for you to make just one mistake and they pounce." (Foster, 1998) The slogans and murals which adorn many walls in Protestant Belfast: 'No Surrender' and 'Yield Not An Inch', increase religious tension and paranoia as each new generation absorbs inflexibility as a virtue.

Mitchell shares, with Parker, a keen sense of humour that those under siege often develop. In the past, it had been the Nationalist community that felt under siege from an oppressive Protestant Unionist government. Irish Nationalism has now trivialised the Protestant culture, according to Mitchell, making it negative and foreign. Nationalist and Southern Irish perceptions of Ulster Protestants are often simplistic caricatures, but within Unionism and Protestantism there is great diversity. There are several Unionist parties and many different Protestant religious denominations disagreeing with each other. The strength of Ulster Protestantism, with its tradition of independence and individualism, is also very often its weakness. In the past, Protestant employers had been very willing to exploit divisions within their community for their own gains.

Protestants once dominated Northern Ireland as leading business owners and political leaders, but that balance of power had shifted towards a more equitable society where both religious communities play an equal role in a non-discriminatory environment. In Rathcoole, Protestants have increasingly bunkered into a ghetto. The population of Rathcoole has decreased from 20,000 to 10,000 in the past twenty years and has gone from being religiously and economically mixed to being almost exclusively Protestant. Mitchell explains: "Growing up, there was this idea that there was a monster outside your community, and so we never left ... We stayed in Rathcoole, and there's not a lot to do, there are nine churches, two clubs, and a few underground social clubs, that's all. We'd go to the cinema when we were really little, but then that all stopped because people were being bombed and shot all over the place." (Fricker, 55)

Mitchell's plays are a direct result of his desire to get his side of the story out to the world. As a spokesman he's hardly an apologist, and could never be accused of whitewashing as he paints a portrait of a pitch-black, closed system in which there is little hope of escape or change. Each of the plays leads to a crisis point in which the central characters are faced with a decision between political and family loyalty, with either option involving sacrifice or betrayal.

There is a perspective in which anger is a precious thing in any class-divided society, but what is wrong with the wrath fuelling the violence in Northern Ireland is the target it is aimed at. The air is felt thickest with sectarian threat in the places where the lower orders lurk, and the poorer you are, the more likely you are to live in an area where there is only one religion, and usually in an urban, socially-deprived environment. No component of the day-to-day bleakness ordinarily overlaps into shared experience with people similarly situated on the other side. This lack of shared experience is the reason for more rage, and is more likely to burn with enclosed sectarian intensity: "In the leafy glades of south Belfast or behind the picture-windows, necklaced around the shores of north Down, folk can be somewhat more at ease with themselves, and with the variegated ways of the world. It is a question of class that is not a much-discussed concept anymore, but then neither is a dispassionate appraisal. Class has always been and remains a major determinant of Northern Irish political attitudes. It is from the dialectic of class, community and State that finally the answer will come." (McCann, 1998)

In a Little World of Our Own and *As the Beast Sleeps* both focus on an extended working-class family. *As the Beast Sleeps* takes place during a ceasefire and shows a community which had thrived on anti-Catholic violence now suddenly idle and turning in on itself. The plays are set in the Rathcoole estate as it struggles to cope with the shifting circumstances in contemporary Northern Ireland through the cycles of violence and oppression. Mitchell writes brilliantly observed thrillers about these changing circumstances: "The way I see it, you have politicians arguing about this point or that one on a television programme, but who really listens to that? After five minutes you switch off. But in this area of entertainment you can really pull people in; people will be entertained and then they will be forced to think about what they have seen. Realistically, what you have to hope for is that you will not beat the people over the head with some big message but that you make it feel like life itself. Northern Ireland is a confusing place; it is hugely complex, there is no blueprint for a perfect world here." (Fricker, 56)

Just like the state itself, Rathcoole estate was constructed with a distinctive communal sense of identity which conferred on it an official status of sorts, expressed, most conspicuously, in the disdaining of the identity of the Catholic estate one mile down the road: "To the extent that deprivation in life in Rathcoole gave growth to individuals and organisations filled with furious hatred of Catholics, it has been the State and the class in control of the State which contrived it so, and having contrived it, the State then disowned it and provided amplification for pleas to 'the men of violence' to scramble up and join the decent folks on higher and more comfortable ground." (McCann 1998)

Independent Voice (1993), Mitchell's first play for the stage, was performed by the Tinderbox Theatre Company in Belfast. The play focuses on two young newspaper reporters running a small community newspaper, in a ramshackle office, with very different ambitions for themselves and their publication. It is an uncompromising insight into the pressure, in a Belfast community, from those who try to live by their principles. When the two reporters publish their first major story, they find themselves embroiled in an underworld of corruption that begins to threaten their business, their friendship, and their lives. The reporters become increasingly isolated in a close-knit community where betrayal and deception are part of everyday life. All journalists face the same pressures in any part of the world where there is violent conflict. *Independent Voice* is specific to the pressures that journalists face in Belfast and does not name a specific paramilitary organisation.

Summer workshops for young people from Catholic and Protestant schools in Armagh, Northern Ireland, resulted in the script *Made in Heaven* (1996) for the camera. The play revolves around a group of young people who take over a house for a party, in the hope of getting the two central characters, Mary and Kevin, back together again. Things go disastrously wrong when Kevin shows up with someone else. BBC Northern Ireland's Education Unit, through its *Study Ireland: English and Drama* series, made the script possible. The teenagers who developed the storyline played their own characters in the film. The success of the Armagh series led to further BBC projects with young people in Derry and Belfast.

Mitchell's major published works include *In a Little World of Our Own*, *Tearing the Loom* and *Trust*. *In a Little World of Our Own* premiered at the Peacock Theatre in Dublin in 1997 and in London, at the Donmar Warehouse, in 1998. The play was, according to Mitchell, written from the hard hand: "I didn't have to research this play because it is in me." In its boldly uncompromising examination of what it means to belong to a family of loyalists in modern-day Belfast, it vividly reflects the necessity of seeing life from both sides of the equation no matter how unpalatable it might be. Sam Thompson's play *Over the Bridge* also reflected many unpalatable aspects of life in Northern Ireland in his plea for working-class solidarity against sectarianism.

In a Little World of Our Own, set in Rathcoole, declares its tragic intentions by following the classical unities: in a single action, the destruction of three brothers, played out in a single place, in the garish sitting room of their house, over a single day. As in Greek tragedy all of the events—beating, rape and murder—all take place offstage. Walter acts as both Chorus, filling in offstage details as he prompts the action by laying out the alternatives, and as a messenger, bringing word to and from the paramilitary leadership. The play never leaves this political context and, at one level, it is almost an allegory of paramilitarism. Forces that are felt in the public world, as well as the private, which resorts to irrational violence when the survival of the family is threatened, drive the action.

The play takes place in an enclosed world where amoral pragmatism, enveloped in intimidation and violence, seems normal. It is a world in which familial loyalties and love must be expressed in societal chaos and the mere possibility of survival: "Gary Mitchell makes clear that this is not a normal world in which actions are governed by moral or legal imperatives. The problems of Northern Ireland are not just concerned with politics and religion as it is one of the most conservative communities in Western Europe in which family and tribe are at the centre of life. Violence is often more about settling family feuds than Republican dreams of a united Ireland or loyalist insistence on preserving the status quo." (O'Toole, 1997, February)

Mitchell's script is tightly contained and unveils the machismo loyalties and axiomatic sectarianism in a society distrustful of police. Ray is the UDA 'hard man', Richard is his mentally slow younger brother, and Gordon, the eldest, is about to jump into a God-fearing marriage. Major events take place offstage, their mother lies dying, a girl is raped and murdered, and her father, a former paramilitary, turned politician, is clamouring for vengeance.

The action takes place in a house where the conversation is about employment in Shorts Aircraft Factory, once regarded as the 'entitlement' place of work for working-class Protestants. Ray, the terrorist, tells his younger brother as they discuss a game of poker: "It is better to lose the odd time than to lose the odd limb." In games with far higher stakes, they find themselves dragged into a situation where losing a limb can be considered getting off lightly. The brutal compact drama, of mutant morals, shows the three brothers clinging to the family home, the refuge of their dying mother, as their world turns more hostile. Their biggest problem is that violence is not just something that surrounds them, but an activity in which they all, to various degrees, take part. Throughout the play the talk is of broken bones and appropriate punishments and turns to the finer points of extracting confessions, and the video equipment needed to record them.

Walter and Ray are involved in the paramilitary organisation and when they are not tugging at the threads of the loyalist ceasefire, to test whether it is unravelling, they are pondering the Department of Social Security regulations to see what loans and grants they are entitled to. Ray is a freelance operator who spurns the local loyalist paramilitary, whereas Walter is the mysterious black-jacketed 'fixer' who negotiates between the family and the brutal Monroe, the military godfather: "Things are getting out of hand," Walter keeps repeating, like a Beckett refrain, as justice has little meaning, and what matters is showing the community that family honour will be preserved. He warns Gordon:

> In situations like this it's not a case of what should be done—it's about what people feel should be done ... Why should two of your brothers be punished? And in trying to get Richard who else might get hurt? You have other people to think about. Not least your pretty girlfriend. Ever heard of an eye for an eye? (50)

All of the characters in the play are affected, to varying degrees, by violence or the threat of violence, through everyday activities of card playing, praying and talking. The brothers exist primarily as individual vehicles for a moral debate, as the darker heart of the play looms, and they collectively amplify the very human drama coursing through the play's themes: power struggles, emotional isolation, life-threatening violence and the futility of hope. Ray is willing to commit atrocities and his belief that violence works allows him to rush to kill an innocent Catholic to save his own family from the consequences of his own brutality. Richard, the mentally weak brother, is accused of rape and is protected by Ray, while Gordon, the oldest brother, is trying desperately to make a new life for himself away from the violent working-class life of the housing estate, with Deborah, his devout Christian fiancée. They are also willing to turn a blind eye to protect Richard, whose innocence is fatally contaminated by Ray's ferociously controlling love. Two of the characters do not appear on stage: the mother who is ill in bed upstairs, and Susan, the Catholic teenage girl brutally assaulted and raped. What happens to Susan is at the core of the play.

"Tragedies tend to be written at very specific times and in very particular places and to write one you need to be able to draw on a society that is caught between two worlds. You need the chance to imagine people who are so divided within themselves between one world and the other that whatever they do will be wrong and tragedy seldom emerges from utterly bleak circumstances. If there is no change and no hope, as in Northern Ireland for almost thirty years, many plays are grim, sad and violent, but you can't get the tragic tension, the idea that there are credible grounds for hope that will in the course of the action, be blighted. In that sense, Gary Mitchell's play, though it is dark and sombre, is a tentative sign that something has changed. The dashing of hopes that it enacts implies at least that there was in the first place some possibility of hope being fulfilled." (O'Toole, 1997, February)

In a Little World of Our Own is concerned with polarities in the Protestant community and central characters are either Born Again Christians or paramilitaries. Mitchell comments: "The struggle between the brothers over Richard begins ... and really it's my investigation into the struggles between the two, because I believe that it is one of the debates which is happening in Protestantism at the minute. People are beginning to look at the extremities and some obvious decisions need to be made ... The church is pulling them in one direction and the paramilitary are pulling them in another." (Mooney, 1997)

The performance in the Peacock Theatre "was an utterly compelling piece of theatre and for all the bleakness of the action, an oddly hopeful one. If it is true that terrible events can only really be seen when they are over, then the relentlessness of Gary Mitchell's gaze and the quality of his vision suggest that his play may, in its own way, mark a beginning of the end." (O'Toole, 1997, February) Mitchell believed that real efforts to improve the organisations, and to dignify them, suggested they were moving away from violence. If the Protestants of Rathcoole are unwilling to let anyone else tell their story, they have given that freedom to a playwright and one of their own. Mitchell has devoted his writing career to portraying, in often harsh and uncompromising terms, a community besieged by fear and mistrust. He acknowledges that the authenticity and truthfulness of *In a Little World of Our Own* stems directly from personal experience: "I am a working-class Protestant who grew up in a family of active loyalism. As a family we made the journey of going through the fact that violence and the armed struggle are not the way forward. And that represents the current struggle in Protestantism." (Coyle, 1997)

Tearing the Loom shares with Parker's *Northern Star* a re-telling of the struggle of the United Irishmen. Mitchell, in his re-telling of 1798, moves away from the culture and vernacular of modern day urban Belfast. *Tearing the Loom* looks at how the events of 1798 affect the Moore family. The father, Robert Moore, does not want involvement in the sectarian conflict, but his children are divided in their respective loyalties. His daughter, Ruth, fights for the United Irishmen with her lover Harry, and his son David sides against the rebellion.

Set in rural Tandragee, the Protestant family divided against itself in *Tearing the Loom* is caught in a cycle of tribal warfare. The prologue opens with Samuel Hamill, Grand Master of the new lodge, bullying his son to strangle a trussed Catholic woman but also hopes that she was a Presbyterian traitor as they are one and the same in his eyes. The other family in the play, the Moores, are local linen weavers and smallholders, whose son David decides to join the Orangemen.

The farmers in county Armagh in 1798 had ten-acre holdings and made a living from flax and weaving during a period of liberty, the Rights of Man, sectarian suspicion and revolution. The Orange Order had been founded to protect the Protestant community from outside influences and to fight for freedom that had been inspired by the American War of Independence and the French Revolution.

Tearing the Loom explodes outwards and reaches into the past to explore its legacy in the present. The play imaginatively recreates a time and place where history was first inscribed with sectarian blood and divisive hatred between Catholics and Protestants, and Protestants with each other. *Tearing the Loom* is about families, friends and personal conflicts that are distanced from the main action of the 1798 rebellion. The nuanced ideologies of Henry Joy McCracken in Belfast, and Wolfe Tone in Dublin, have little impact on their lives. The opposing ideological forces of the rebellion are those particularly loyal to the crown, to a nation, to a people and to God and history.

"The scope of Mitchell's play is epic, as much as dramatised history, but its focus is also intimate and its resonances are contemporary. Though written primarily as a drama of ideas, *Tearing the Loom* unfolds as a story of a family caught up in events that it is powerless to resist and which will ultimately destroy them. The language of the play is muscular and lean and combines religious rhetoric with contemporary vernacular to simultaneously evoke the past it describes and renders immediate with history dissolved into the dramatic present." (Clarke, 1998)

Tearing the Loom is Mitchell's first play that moves away from the urban working-class environment: "I was struck by a remark that Wolfe Tone was supposed to have made that, if his movement failed, it would set Ireland back two hundred years. I am now living two hundred years later, so where does that put us? Back to the time when Tone was trying to change things ... things have changed so little." (Coyle, 1998) Mitchell repeats, wearily, that the killing still goes on and in *Tearing the Loom*, many scenes are full of powerful, dramatic cruelty.

Tearing the Loom is dramatically flawed, as there is little attempt to capture a distinctive language of the period. Parker inherited the great gifts of Anglo-Irish theatricality and in *Northern Star*, he captured the period of the late eighteenth-century Ireland through a creative and imaginative use of language, missing in *Tearing the Loom*. Mitchell has been unable to find the creative distancing which is required to make a more composite work for the theatre: "While allowing the echoes of history to sound in the present, he draws taut the threads between the bloody deeds, of two centuries ago, and the present day, but the dramatic element fails. *In a Little World of Our Own* succeeded in painting a picture that contained many shades of grey in contrast to *Tearing the Loom*, which is a stark monochrome. Drama becomes melodrama when blood begins to spill, and in the closing scenes in *Tearing the Loom* our suspended belief comes crashing down on top of us." (McFadden, 1998)

The passionate focus on the message in *Tearing the Loom* means the medium has been neglected. After the success of *In a Little World of Our Own*, critics were less than enthusiastic about *Tearing the Loom* as it wavered between historical drama and allegory. As a young playwright, with many successes during the 1990s, Mitchell had taken a risk with *Tearing the Loom* and as most of the critics also suggest, the play might have fared better under a more accomplished director. The premiere at the Lyric Theatre was disappointing and lost the power that Mitchell's earlier works had sustained in menace-filled portrayals of urban Belfast life.

The first act of the play becomes laboriously schematic as Mitchell tries to establish the political background, the family microcosms and their neatly conflicting allegiances. The second act follows a more remorseless dramatic logic that, if directed well, might have avoided the melodrama that many of the play's critics denounced. In *Tearing the Loom*, Mitchell's angry despair and hatred of the men of violence in the final scenes leaves no sense of hope, and without hope there will be no future for Northern Ireland.

While in London, Mitchell acknowledged that in writing for a wider audience during his residency at the Royal National Theatre, he would need to broaden the scope and appeal of his plays. Stewart Parker had also written about the role of the Northern Irish playwright and the dangers of writing within the narrow confines of the Troubles. In Parker's terms the playwright should elevate the craft of playwriting in Northern Ireland and broaden the playwright's canvas into a wider universal context, including Irish sensibility, humour, tragedy and absurdity.

Mitchell's eighteenth play, and his fifth for the stage, *As the Beast Sleeps*, is another stark cautionary thriller set in his native Rathcoole. The play was the second of Mitchell's works to be premiered at The Peacock and dispelled the doubts expressed about his work after the controversial *Tearing the Loom* run at the Lyric Theatre. *As the Beast Sleeps* is a brutal portrayal of life in Rathcoole and more startlingly accomplished than its predecessor. The shock value of graphic brutality was part of the success of *In a Little World of Our Own* in the south of Ireland. Audiences in Dublin could afford to be smug because it was loyalist in nature, which served to disguise some glaring structural and textual weaknesses. (O'Kelly, 1998)

As the Beast Sleeps, although different from its predecessor *In a Little World of Our Own* in many respects, is similar to it in some. The brutality of paramilitary justice is as graphic, but the real horror lies in the depiction of the mindset where the characters inhabit a world of ethical nightmare in which murder by torture is admirable 'for the cause'. Mitchell has refined his characters; they are people with diverse motivations and real lives to be destroyed by fear, violence, hatred and ignorance. As the play pitches action against words and manages to be discursive without being didactic. Mitchell locates the ideological conflict in the everyday world of his characters. These characters again come from working-class Rathcoole but they are also more complex than in previous plays. There is a greater confidence and sophistication in Mitchell's writing that has attained an authenticity that allows for an extensive shading of the truth.

Politicians and some churchmen in Northern Ireland, whether newly arrived or of long-standing involvement in the democratic process, have often reiterated the view that there is no longer any justification for violence. Believers in real democracy know that there never was, and that violence is its own justification and the only one. "The dominance of reason over myth and tradition is a philosophy that has been slowly refined over the two hundred years since the Age of Reason. But where religion or tribalism has dominated, intellectual rationalism has always been slow to gain a foothold. Brought to a logical conclusion that bodes ill for Ireland where religion and politics are still virtually indistinguishable from each other and this is Gary Mitchell's gloomy view of Northern Ireland." (O'Kelly, 1998)

What is of interest to Mitchell is not the peace process so much as the war process and the indelible marks of militarisation on the community. "*As the Beast Sleeps* is a drama about war and politics, and the manoeuvres that might allow some people to move profitably between the two, but will leave many others stranded and angry. The first act follows these manoeuvres with high energy and emotional explosiveness. Some of the argumentativeness in the first act is couched in authentically articulate language, which seems, at times, to curl in on itself and impede the narrative process and could benefit dramatically from some careful pruning." (Nowland, 1998)

The dramatic plot in the second act begins with mordant humour as a maelstrom of events increases with terrifying intensity. It may not answer all the questions raised about loyalism and loyalty, friendship and belief, change and uncertainty, but it is a compelling work for the theatre that provides an extraordinary insight into human conflict. The action revolves around a clandestine drinking club, and typically, Mitchell exposes corrupt hegemonies, class divides and the secretive command structures endemic in Northern Ireland. Politicians, paramilitary organisations, and vigilante factions are all crumbling under the pressure of the peace process.

Those who were once active in the paramilitary organisations are now finding it difficult to readjust to life as the peace process begins to unfold and their status in the community is no longer certain. Kyle and Freddie were members of a paramilitary organisation and when the conflict was at its height they had a role to play, and status, within the community. When the ceasefire began in 1995 they found it difficult to come to terms with the fact that paramilitarism was also changing. The paramilitary organisations had to begin the process of legitimising their activities as the drinking clubs, which had gone underground, had to find a means of living in a society without violence, where the legitimate forces of law and order would, it was hoped, resume authority. For over thirty years at the local level, and particularly with the urban working class, the paramilitary organisations had dictated their own terms for law and order.

During the opening scenes in the play, the respectable politician, Alec, promises the UDA activist, Larry, a position in politics if he brings the renegades into the peace process. Larry, in turn, leans on Kyle to bring in the diehard activists who refuse to lay down their arms. Kyle suggests that a 'knee capping' gang may be employed to help him in his mission. He must also bring his best friend, Freddie, a volatile and perpetually nervous hotheaded activist, into the peace process. This leads to a climactic and violent confrontation following the robbery of an Ulster club in which Freddie is the chief suspect. The peace agreement is in place, the guns have been silenced and for large numbers of unemployed working-class Protestants, their *raison d'être* has been removed. Nothing has replaced the void, as the UDA terrorists have no active role in defending Ulster against a common enemy, the Irish Republican Army. When the ballot box finally replaces the bomb and bullet, society has to engage with the paramilitary men who are no longer regarded as heroes.

Kyle and Freddie are long-standing buddies when we discover them scraping wallpaper in the barely furnished living room of Kyle's house where he lives with his wife Sandra and their young son Joe. They had been members of an active, young team, in a loyalist paramilitary organisation and had enjoyed their activities, whether murder or theft, because they believed that everything they did was in the cause of defending Protestant Ulster. Things were simple in the war, Protestants were the 'good' men and 'Taigs' (Catholics) were the bad guys. As the peace process has begun and illegal activities have

[177]

stopped, Kyle and Freddie are now trying desperately to clean up their clandestine activities. Things are far from simple, as opinions and attitudes fragment in wild verbal and physical conflicts between the former members of the active unit. Kyle and Freddie believe the peace process will not lead anywhere, but Kyle is prepared to conform to the new strategies, while Freddie asserts that it will allow the old enemy to regroup and destroy unionism with its defences down.

As their world falls apart, more venal men than Freddie and Kyle move opportunistically with the times to reap the good life, by re-packaging their predatory exploitation of their own community, by calling their financial and social plundering a peace dividend. Kyle comments: "Taigs hate us, and we hate them; that's the way it's always been, and that's the way it's going to stay." When hatred is accepted as a way of life, tragedy is the only result and *As the Beast Sleeps* is a succinct and terrible biblical denouement of brother turning on brother. Freddie, angered by Kyle's acceptance of the peace process and the inaction of the paramilitaries, begins to lose his sense of self, calming himself down only by the occasional brawl. He would be much happier to return to a more satisfying occupation in the paramilitary unit. Freddie wants to do something and do it now: the peace process and progress mean nothing as they confuse and frustrate him. Everyone is telling him he has to change as there will be no more jobs stealing cigarettes and booze, no more killing Catholics and in fact nothing as it was before. Freddie is powerless to do anything about it and is angry and alone. Mitchell struggles with the political and cultural effects of the peace process in his play and his characters embody the emotional and psychological fall-out of that process.

The play is a searing portrait of a man, Kyle, who is being strangled by the chain of command and who is clever enough to know that old loyalties are not enough when the tenor of the time has changed. Freddie, on the other hand, is both a violent bigot and a sympathetic human being who believes the politicians have 'sold out'. The play puts his case without distortion, even if we understand, like Kyle, that the tide will not be turned back by old methods. The choice is a simple one, go with the flow or become a renegade; a political and personal conundrum that exists on both sides of Northern Ireland's sectarian divide.

As the Beast Sleeps is a timely reminder that loyalism and nationalism are as similar, and as far apart, as ever. The end of the play returns to where it began, in a torture room, as the cycle of beatings continue. Mitchell, in a brutal close-up of the appalling costs of shaking off the past, shows that even the closest of friends suddenly come to fear and distrust each other.

Claustrophobic in its intensity, the action in the Dublin premiere was played out in the tight rooms of Blaithin Sherrin's revolving set, spinning between a crimson torture chamber and a suburban living room. The infusion of visceral energy and force of the actors' physical precision, and emotional vulnerability, was palpable from the Peacock ensemble. Conall Morrison's direction combined extraordinary physical and emotional intensity that shaped and released the dramatic intensity that coursed throughout the play, making it a compelling and memorable piece of theatre.

Trust (1999) was commissioned by the Royal National Theatre and premiered at the Royal Court Theatre Upstairs by the English Stage Company. The background for *Trust* is once again Mitchell's home territory, Rathcoole, and was the first of his plays to have been performed in the United States. Mitchell has criticised the romantic views of Ireland on the New York stage: "The Protestant culture sees the whole Irish movement as one big machine that churns out this romantic nonsense over and over. There is no organisation, no machine to promote my community, to say anything about the political situation here, in an even-handed way, therefore my work gets shelved or pushed aside ... The problem right now is that the two sides have always looked to someone else to support them, the Catholics to the

[179]

Irish and further afield to America, and the Protestants obviously to Britain. Now it is like the teacher has left the school yard and we are on our own and the reaction is naturally fear and violence ... " (Fricker, 1998)

In June 2000, *Marching On* was premiered at the Lyric Theatre as the Orange marching season was preparing for its annual 1690 celebrations. The play is an exploration of the marching season as seen through the eyes of three loyalist generations.

Northern Ireland is bracing itself for the Drumcree March that had been banned by the Parades Commission, a decision unacceptable to the Orange Lodge. Grandfather Samuel is an Orangeman, his son Christopher is an officer in the Royal Ulster Constabulary and his grandson Ricky is a young thug who is happy to burn cars and riot, but cries when his mother rejects him. The lines between peaceful protest and street violence are blurred but as the play progresses, it becomes clear who the enemy is and how the Parades Commission could resolve the March to everyone's satisfaction.

Marching On explores the dynamics of loyalist ideology and politics in a domestic context. Divisions between father and son and between brother and brother serve to highlight the divisions in the loyalist community where women witness rather than participate in the warring factions. The familial, allied to evangelical, impulses in the play anchor Mitchell's polemics in a recognisable human situation.

Samuel, a high-ranking member of the Orange Lodge, helps to organise a silent vigil along the police barricades, as a peaceful protest against the Parades Commission decision to ban their Drumcree march. His grandson, the angry and hot-headed Ricky, wants to burn the 'Taigs' out and joins in night attacks on Catholic homes in Drumcree. A fifteen-year old boy is used as a personal battleground by his paramilitary father and his intransigent mother, as he becomes the product of a divided home and culture. Christopher, Ricky's father, is a member of the recently reformed Police Service of Northern Ireland and is caught in the middle of the Protestant protests where he must uphold the law and protect the Catholic families against his own people. The Scottish visitor, Johnny, serves the plot as an uncomprehending outsider.

David Ervine, a Progressive Unionist Party member of the Northern Ireland Assembly, argued that *Marching On* is more than relevant in the present political climate. He acknowledged that Mitchell does not offer any answers to the nightmare of violence and contends that *Marching On* adds no new dimension to the Ulster situation: "What is acknowledged in the play is that Mitchell is trying to force the debate and for this reason it was hoped that more working-class people would see the play and understand it as a building block and a glimpse of times of change." (Ervine, 2000)

The problems that beset Northern Ireland are generational as well as sectarian and in Mitchell's persuasive view the divided families are a metaphor for a divided community, and as in all of his previous plays, no one has the monopoly on truth. Mitchell accepts that Orange and Green have their own separate values but in his complex world there are no simple black and white answers. It is his ability to convey the contradictions of the Protestant community that makes Gary Mitchell a major writer. As well as conveying the Protestant paradox of love for the Crown, but hatred of the English, he also fulfils one of drama's most basic functions which is the anthropological recording of the country's customs. *Marching On* "lacks the formal adventurousness of his earlier work and especially in the more recent *Force of Change*, but it is vibrantly informative. A Unionist politician remarked that the strengths of writers like Mitchell and Marie Jones is that they record Northern Ireland's tribal divisions from the inside but with a critical eye." (Billington, 2000) Local critics were less sanguine about the Lyric production of *Marching On* and questioned the validity of Mitchell's work and its contemporary relevance. They felt the play was a little overwritten for home audiences who are all too aware of the nuances and shifts in the political foreplay on the eve of the marching season.

Mitchell is one of the most prolific dramatists in Ireland and certainly one of the most successful. His success has resulted in work that is both commercially and creatively successful. Writing, for Mitchell, is a two-way process: "It's not just about me churning out the same stuff; it's what people want. My problem is that when I pitch ideas for plays that aren't about Protestants, nobody picks them up. I would like to deal with all kinds of human behaviour problems and not just those of Northern Ireland Protestants, but I think it's a good place to start. We have so much debate and conflict in our lives. It's a good foundation to talk about the world." (McFadden, 2000)

If there is a motif in Mitchell's work, it is about bringing about change and the fear and occasional opportunity it brings. He has been accused of writing for a specific Protestant audience and yet of pandering to a Catholic audience. The reality is that Mitchell writes plays that have specific locations, and writing about a particular community does not prevent him from introducing universal themes and applying them to that community. *Marching On* is an accurate portrait of a Unionist community tearing itself apart.

The Protestant population grew up with the myth that because they were Protestant they were necessarily 'better off' than Catholics. Mitchell claims that he was betrayed by this myth as he realised that it was about self-perception and that he had depended on the myth and then felt betrayed by it. These perceived betrayals led to a more favourable perception of the Nationalist community internationally and added to the Unionist siege mentality. In over forty works for the stage, screen and radio, Mitchell has responded to these perceived betrayals both positively and prodigiously as he has engaged the outside world with an unabashedly working-class Ulster Protestant perspective, rarely seen on stage, and which also attacks critically the many Unionist shibboleths. "Ultimately drawn to an egalitarian independent Northern Ireland, Mitchell has stated that he has resisted advice to take a more commercially acceptable Nationalist slant in his work and is especially concerned that a forthcoming film version of *As the Beast Sleeps* should not be given a green hue." (Heaney M., 2000)

Mitchell's work has received critical acclaim in London, but in his native Belfast, audiences and critics have been less enthusiastic. The mirror that Mitchell holds up to the Protestant community is one which does not reflect the desired image. By exposing the underworld of the Rathcoole paramilitaries, a crack has begun to appear in one of the bastions of Protestant hegemony. The pre-Protestant marching season in June 2000 saw poor audiences for *Marching On* at the Lyric Theatre in Belfast. Possibly if Mitchell's work was performed in community theatres, where audiences would see themselves reflected on stage, his plays might have a larger impact in Northern Ireland.

Since December 2005, Mitchell and his extended family have been in hiding in Northern Ireland after a campaign of death threats and bomb attacks by loyalist paramilitaries. He has been branded a 'traitor' by many in his own community. "Remarkably, while critics raved at the way he dramatised feuds and power-struggles within the loyalist gangs, and the collusion between gunmen and the police, he managed to continue living on the same streets where they held sway. Despite police warnings that he was on the top of a death list, and should not drink in local pubs, Mitchell insisted on staying put, saying he needed to be close to the people he was writing about ... The paramilitaries' prejudice that culture was something only for 'taigs and faggots' protected him. But after his acclaimed *As the Beast Sleeps* was filmed by the BBC, and he began to win international prizes, it began to get serious." (Chrisafis, 2005)

Mitchell shares, with Marie Jones, an early introduction to the stage through the Belfast Youth Theatre and also an active participation in community theatre. Jones began her work as a playwright through Charabanc, which had a collaborative working method, but eventually Jones became the primary playwright for the company. Whereas Mitchell honed his plays on a Protestant community in north Belfast, Jones has a more flexible talent as she has produced work that has travelled easily between both communities and played at community centres across the divided city. Jones has also expressed some of the anger found in Mitchell's plays but it is more internalised, it is confrontational but controlled. In the following chapter, I will examine Jones' early work with Charabanc, her working method in collaborative theatre and her present success on the international stage.

CHAPTER SIX

Marie Jones
Refiguring the Theatrical Landscape

Marie Jones belongs to the second generation of Northern Irish playwrights, after Sam Thompson, and shares with Thompson and Parker a Protestant, east Belfast, background. Jones' output has been prolific over the past eighteen years with plays for theatre, television and radio. Her work is informed by her background in a wry, self-effacing humour, and sardonic insight into the mind of the northern Protestant.

Jones has been writing plays that focus beyond the Troubles of Northern Ireland and include a broad human interest. Whereas Mitchell's dramatic world is working-class, masculine, and brutal, Jones' is middle-class, feminine and comic. Both Mitchell and Jones became playwrights by working with improvisational theatres, Jones with Charabanc, the Lyric and Belfast Youth Theatres and Mitchell with the Belfast Youth Theatre. They came to the theatre not through literature (as Parker did) but through performance workshops that draw as much on popular culture, and the media, for dramatic models as on any literary tradition.

Theatres in Ireland have ignored many Irish women writers. Jones does not, however, regard herself as a feminist writer and would probably agree with the American poet Elizabeth Bishop, who objected on principle to appearing in a women's anthology:

"Undoubtedly gender does play an important part in the making of any art, but art is art and to separate writings, paintings, musical compositions etc. into two sexes is to emphasise values in them that are not art." (Williams, 6)

There have been many important plays by Irish women during the last three decades. Marie Jones explored women's themes in a number of plays, including *The Hamster Wheel* (1990), *Women on the Verge of HRT* (1996), and *Ruby* (2000) which charters the life of the famous Belfast chanteuse Ruby Murray of whom Jones has stated: "It was a wonderful story to tell. Her background was not unlike mine and I came to know the world which became her world, the world of showbiz with all its high spots and disappointments, the way she reached the top and the later decline." (Love, 24)

Jones' writing for the theatre over the past twenty-four years includes *Lay Up Your Ends* (1984), *Oul Delf and False Teeth* (1984), *Now You're Talkin'* (1985), *Ethel Workman is Innocent* (1995), *Gold in the Streets* (1986), *Girls in the Big Picture* (1986), *Somewhere Over the Balcony* (1987), *The Terrible Twins' Crazy Christmas* (1988), *Under Napoleon's Nose* (1988), *It's a Waste of Time Tracey* (1989), *Weddings, Wee'ins and Wakes* (1989), *The Hamster Wheel* (1990, adapted for television 1991), *The Blind Fiddler of Glenadaugh* (1990), *Hang All the Harpers* (1991), *Hiring Days* (1992), *Don't Look Down* (1992), *Yours Truly* (1993), *A Night in November* (1994), *The Government Inspector* (1995, Adaptation), *Women on the Verge of HRT* (1995), *Stones in His Pockets* (1996), *Eddie Bottom's Dream* (1996), *The Wedding Community Play* (1999), *Ruby* (2000), *Convictions* (2000), *Christmas Eve Can Kill You* (2002), *A Very Weird Manor* (2005). For television: *Tribes* (1990, BBC), *Fighting the Shadows* (1992, Channel 4), *Wingnut and the Sprog* (1994, BBC). Jones' work for the Charabanc Theatre Company during its ten-year existence has been substantially documented. In this chapter, I will briefly examine *Somewhere Over the Balcony*, *The Hamster Wheel*, *A Night in November* and *Stones in His Pockets*, which was produced independently by Jones.

Marie Jones received her education at Orangefield Girls' School in Belfast where there was a tradition of drama taught by the art teacher Joan Rolston. Pupils were greatly influenced by the teaching of Sam McCready and his artistic directorship of the Lyric Theatre and the Lyric Youth Theatre in Belfast. Many young performers of this generation under McCready and Rolston went into professional theatre.

As a member of this generation of fledgling drama students, Jones had also known life in Belfast before the beginning of 'the Troubles' in 1969; a world in which theatre, music, literature and art flourished in Belfast. Life before, and after, 1969 was never the same for anyone from Northern Ireland as the violence had a profound effect on the artistic community. Jones' work is informed by a Belfast sensibility and a rawness that contains the essence of Northern Irish humour and the ability to examine the northern Protestant objectively.

For Jones, no experience was ever extraneous, including her first job in 1966 on the cheese counter at Littlewoods department store in Belfast. It was here she heard the first comments by the Belfast public on the introduction of the continental yogurt, which had by the mid-sixties not yet entered into the local culinary world. The northern Irish vernacular permeates Jones' work, through the tradition of storytelling and humour that is the point of departure for much of her writing.

The Belfast shipyard, where her father worked, influenced family life. Stories of shipyard life, the Second World War and sectarianism all played a major role in Jones' development as playwright and actress. With a warm attachment to Belfast, she has used its distinctive brand of storytelling, in many of her plays, to portray its many contradictions from within the Protestant and Catholic communities with their inherent prejudices and antagonisms. Jones found a means of looking at her own culture objectively through the theatre and after leaving Orangefield Girls' School she worked wherever possible in amateur and professional theatre.

Her first work, in professional theatre, began with the versatile Belfast caricaturist, James Young, at the Ulster Group Theatre, Belfast. She played the juvenile lead in *Little Boxes* that ran for six months. (Love, 23) The Group Theatre became the home of a particular brand of Ulster comedy headed by Young. As chairman of the company, he had stated his desired policy for the Ulster Group Theatre: "It will not be a place of misery and arty-crafty nonsense" and he added that he was opposed to the principle of a company of permanent members as "that could, in my opinion, turn into a repertory company, and actors could be forced to take parts for which they are completely unsuited." (Byrne 49) Young did not explicate what exactly the "arty-crafty nonsense" was.

Jones worked with the Lyric Youth Theatre, the Clarence Players and the Belvoir Players in Belfast. Community theatre was developing in Belfast through the formation of Playzone which toured in a 'double-decker' bus to many of Belfast's working-class neighbourhoods meandering between the peace line dividing the Shankhill and Falls. Jones was one of the first members of the Playzone Theatre Group which experimented with new theatre forms and toured during the summer months in Belfast. Theatres during the 1970s were not well attended as violence deterred audiences from travelling into the city. The Lyric Theatre, because of its location, managed to sustain an audience throughout the most troubled times. Playzone's mission was to take theatre to those who could not travel to the city and to present work that had its roots in the community. For Jones these early experiments with Playzone inspired a community-based theatre that would emerge in 1983 with the formation of Charabanc.

There was occasional work in Belfast's main theatres but Jones, along with other actresses, was frustrated, not only by the lack of work available for women in the theatre, but also the quality of that work. Out of frustration with the established theatre, Jones, Eleanor Methven, Carol Scanlan, Maureen

McAuley and Brenda Winter explored the possibility of producing their own work. With help from Martin Lynch, Charabanc produced its first work *Lay Up Your Ends* (1983). The title of the play referred to the workers in the Belfast Linen Mills where the linen production process involved tying up broken threads. *Lay Up Your Ends* is set in the York Street Mill in 1911 and charts the lives of five women working there. The play documents the two-week strike in 1911, organised by James Connolly. The strike did not succeed in its initial aims of preventing shorter working hours, and therefore less pay, but more importantly for the workers, it resulted in the foundation of the first women's branch of the Irish Transport and General Workers' Union.

Martin Lynch advised the company to begin by looking back at the lives of Ulster women, of the actresses' grandmothers and what life in Belfast had been like for them. All the company members in Charabanc had family connections with the Belfast linen mills and through stories and anecdotal references, the company began to piece together the Women Mill Workers' strike of 1911. Charabanc's early working methods involved researching archive sources, newspaper cuttings and newsreels: "We go and interview people about the subject matter ... We were talking to people, not just about working in mills or being involved in the 1949 election, but about the attitude of the time. We spoke to teachers, doctors, ministers and people from all walks of life to get a clear idea. We had all those tapes and interviews ..."(Jones, 1986) Jones would undertake the writing, with drafts undergoing a collective editing process. As a result, Charabanc's initial plays were collaborative works in which authorship was difficult to pinpoint. *Lay Up Your Ends* was credited to Martin Lynch, Marie Jones and the company.

Charabanc began the writing and exploration for *Lay Up Your Ends* at the Tyrone Guthrie Centre at Annaghmakerrig in Ireland. This experience gave Jones the confidence to write, which she felt had been lacking: "I had never had confidence about spelling, for instance ... Martin Lynch told me to do it phonetically and an obstacle disappeared." (Love, 23) Jones became the principal writer for Charabanc and channelled its energies into originating new work for the theatre and the resultant plays that "explored ways of dealing with the lives of 'insignificant' people, women who are supposed to have no place in history other than as extras for crowd scenes. They [have] forged a kind of wit and fluidity that allows them to deal with oppression without being oppressive, with boredom without being boring, confinement without being confined ... assurance is brought to bear in keeping the balance between enlightenment and entertainment that the material demands." (O'Toole, 1990)

Lay Up Your Ends opened at the Arts Theatre, Belfast, on 15 May, 1983, "to the unfamiliar sight of hundreds of people queuing right down Botanic Avenue". (Coyle, 1984) By October, *Lay Up Your Ends* had been seen by fourteen thousand people in over ninety-six performances, in fifty-nine venues, and the company was credited with having rapidly carved out "a new and comprehensive touring circuit that included both rural and urban venues ... Audiences ranged from farmers and ex-mill women to the arts festival crowds. The appeal to a broader base, one which includes the working classes, became a priority in the company's work." (DiCenzo, 1993)

The members of Charabanc had intended to return to their original professional goals after the production but the success of *Lay Up Your Ends* convinced some of the actresses to continue and a core company emerged, led by Methven, Scanlan and Jones. Between 1983 and 1988 they worked with Pam Brighton, Ian McElhinney, Andy Hinds and Peter Sheridan to stage six new plays by Jones to critical acclaim. *Oul Delf and False Teeth* (1984) was Jones' second play in which she repeated the writing and research process by interviewing people in the community. The play chronicles the disappearing Belfast Variety Markets and the demise of the Northern Ireland Labour Party during the 1949 sectarian election year. Pam Brighton directed the play and helped spawn Jones' international career with Charabanc. The Company toured in October 1984 to Russia, Moscow and St. Petersberg, and to Vilnius, Lithuania, and London for one month at the Drill Hall and the Albany Empire.

Now You're Talkin' (1985), also directed by Pam Brighton, was Jones' third play, and part of the Belfast trilogy. The play takes place in a Northern Ireland reconciliation centre to which five women (Protestant and Catholic) are brought to discover what binds them together. They end up in a more dynamic exploration of what divides them and take the encounter group into their own hands for some straight, honest talking. The play opened at the Belfast Arts Theatre and then began an extensive tour in Northern Ireland and Germany where it represented Northern Ireland at the International Theatre Festival in Munich. The tour continued to the Edinburgh Festival and Toronto, Canada, before returning to London's Drill Hall.

The Girls in the Big Picture (1986) departed from Charabanc's previous concerns with the people and politics of Belfast. The play examines the lives of three spinsters in rural Ulster in 1960 and the parochial attitudes towards unmarried women. The production opened in one of Northern Ireland's newest theatres, the Ardhowen in Enniskillen, with further performances at the Dublin Theatre Festival and a six-week tour of Ireland.

On the eve of the anniversary of the introduction of internment without trial *Somewhere Over the Balcony* (1987) documents life in Belfast's Divis flats, one of the worst public housing projects in Western Europe. Three neighbours live out a single day in their lives at Divis where children hijack and 'joyride' in cars, walls collapse, a cathedral is under siege and a British Army helicopter is hijacked. The play is a black comedy that exposes the reality of survival in the midst of chaos and the dignity of the population under siege. *Somewhere Over the Balcony* was directed by Peter Sheridan and opened in the Drill

Hall in London. The production later toured Northern Ireland and Galway and returned to the Belfast Queen's Festival where it was seen by the residents of Divis flats, who, through their own personal stories, had helped in the creation of the work. In the United States, *Somewhere Over the Balcony* toured to Baltimore, Boston, San Francisco and Minneapolis.

David Nowland, writing about the Dublin Peacock production of *Somewhere Over the Balcony* described it as "one of the most cogent, yet one of the least sane, productions that this inventive group has ever cobbled together". (Nowland, 1987) At this point in her writing career *Somewhere Over the Balcony* was the most controversial subject matter that Jones had tackled. Passions were high in Belfast over the role of the British army in west Belfast and particularly among the angry inhabitants of the Catholic Lower Falls and the Divis Flats. At first sight the flats could have been almost any high-rise, low-income projects in a run-down neighbourhood of any city; the lifts do not work, the plumbing is out of order and the conversation of the day between Ceely, Rose-Marie and Kate is about their disfunctioning environment and bingo. Improbability piles upon unlikelihood, but a crazy authenticity is maintained throughout the play in which the humour is pithy and dark, and incisively unsentimental, as these ordinary people go about their daily lives.

As the three women on stage tell of cars being blown up by controlled explosions, visits by British army helicopters, armed cars patrolling the streets and the slum living conditions, only occasionally does the reality of their existence seep through the humorous veneer. The present reality leaves the question hanging; how can people accept lives so consumed by violence and hopelessness? The same questions are universal and are as potent as those of Soweto, the Gaza strip or any of the many other troubled areas of the world.

Somewhere Over the Balcony is a very effective work of political theatre in which a powerful message is delivered in the guise of entertainment. It is a presentational style of documentary theatre, with music, in which there is little attempt at outright illusion, resembling Brecht's political cabarets. Jones has said that she wrote *Somewhere Over the Balcony* to depict people trying to live normal lives in an abnormal world but plays about Northern Ireland do not need to be airless or weighty diatribes. Jones manages to turn Northern Ireland's bloody civil strife into a wacky war waged by Keystone Kops rather than the British and Irish Republican armies. *Somewhere Over the Balcony* is one of Jones' least realistic plays as "the audience is most obviously encouraged to identify, not with specific characters and events, but rather with material construction that comprises characters and events". (Sullivan, 162)

Charabanc toured throughout the world and to the United States five times. Jones recalls a visit to Baltimore and the World Stage Festival where they brought their props in a battered suitcase and asked what they needed in terms of staging, Jones replied, "A table and four chairs." This was in contrast to many of the other companies performing at the same festival where elaborate sets and scenery had been necessary. This minimalism made touring viable for the company and explains its long existence in the ephemeral world of touring theatre.

After ten years and fifteen productions, the Company decided to cease its operations. By 1988 the core members of Charabanc had reached a point of creative exhaustion and there were also perennial financial difficulties. As the company received funding on a project-by-project basis from the Arts Council, company members were paid solely for performance work and their essential, extensive research time went unpaid. Difficulties had also arisen with funding for community tours. (Byrne, 71) Charabanc's legacy is that it reinvented a form of community theatre and working-class drama in Northern Ireland inspiring many younger companies to follow them. "Now (according to Jones) community arts are flourishing and I'm sure that this is because theatre is a very powerful platform. You are often a voice expressing what people themselves cannot say. People can and do get together now to share common experiences." (Love, 24)

Charabanc provided Jones with a platform to experiment with her own scripts and her subsequent development as an international playwright. Contemporary reviews were often critical of Charabanc, but support for the company and its achievements was unwavering. In a review of *The Girls in the Big Picture*, such support is evident: "Somebody, perhaps the director, should cut the dead wood from this production ... On the other hand, many smoother professional companies must long for the human interest of Charabanc scripts and the honest, sensitive, gritty, explosive acting of the principals." (Smith, 1986)

The Hamster Wheel (1990) was the last Jones play performed by Charabanc Theatre Company and was first staged at the Arts Theatre, Belfast, with other performances at the Riverside Studios, London. *The Hamster Wheel*, based on extensive interviews and research, examines 'other' troubles in Northern Ireland. The play asserts Jones' position as an fully-fledged established playwright and inaugurated the next decade of her writing that would establish her work on the international stage. *The Hamster Wheel* is deeply compassionate and confidently nudges farce out of tragedy: "It allows itself a sentimental response where a sentiment is the most honest response ... The play demonstrates the unique social and emotional perceptions that inform Marie's work and indicate at some point in the near future that Marie will write a major play." (Brighton, 1990)

The characters in *The Hamster Wheel* are astutely observed studies of ordinary people in extraordinary situations. The humour of the previous plays is still there, but at the heart of the play is a mixture of tragedy and comedy as members of the Duncan family try to cope with the sudden and debilitating illness of Kenny Duncan. "The play captures the strength and weaknesses of the 'Ulster Male' and, for that matter, of the

'Ulster Female'. The characters are individual, but they are also tellingly typical." (Grant, 1990)

Kenny and Jeanette Duncan are in their early forties when Kenny, "a big loud-mouthed long-distance truck driver", suffers a severe stroke that leaves him physically and psychologically paralysed. As she approaches this frequently ignored social problem, Jones delves into dark marital recesses that people do not ordinarily discuss. The play compellingly documents the round-the-clock nursing of a loved one. Kenny, who once drove his truck all over Europe, is now permanently at home and taken care of by his wife, who feels guilty if she has to leave him to go to the shop. The logistical difficulties of their situation are dramatised as moral conflicts arising from the instinctive desire to do everything possible to help a physically disabled loved one. This is counterpoised in most of us by the feeling that we still owe at least something to ourselves. Without ever dismissing the tragedy of Kenny's situation, the play centres on Jeanette's dilemma as she is forced to leave her job as a school meals supervisor, to become a full-time care giver.

Cathy, their daughter, is a part of the maternal mix as she faces pressure from Jeanette to postpone her scholarship journey to Germany to help look after her father. We can sympathise with Cathy's position, as she needs to proceed with her plans to leave for Germany and to "psyche herself up to make the decision by brooding over old and unjust resentments against a dad whose shyness before his educated daughter she has misinterpreted as indifference. On the other hand, her uncle's sententious contempt for her won't do either. It is interesting that he, the play's most voluble advocate of self-sacrifice, is also the one figure whose self remains completely unsacrificed." (Taylor, 1990)

The Hamster Wheel is the story of Jeanette's new job. The day Kenny returns from hospital she becomes a full-time care giver but she has no job description, no information and no idea of what lies ahead of her. She is equipped only with her love for

Kenny and a feeling of responsibility that is her only armour against her feelings of fear and bewilderment. As time passes she experiences anger, resentment, frustration and guilt until she arrives at a level of understanding and acceptance in making choices which others find incomprehensible. The obvious victim of this story is Kenny, but the play is about Jeanette as she is the victim of guilt, love and duty, she is what 'Community Care' means in practice. *The Hamster Wheel* asks us what burdens we have chosen to carry, or those we have foisted upon us and for the hundreds of thousands of care givers whose burden is human, tangible and practical. In Ireland there is an accepted tradition of care being given by another family member. Jeanette's sister Patsy and her husband Norman also face a dilemma as Patsy, in due course, will also be expected to look after Norman's ageing mother. Jeanette's imprisoning predicament only adds to Patsy's determination that she will not become a primary care giver. *The Hamster Wheel* is a portrait of a living hell, from Jeanette's devastating loss, to her need for male company and finally to her freedom. The play is as finely dramatic as its metaphoric title suggests, although the title is the play's sole metaphor. Everything else in the play is unadorned realism that is appropriate, given the emotion and power of the play's central subject.

After her departure from Charabanc in 1990, Jones began writing for Dubbeljoint Productions whose director, Pam Brighton, had also been involved with Charabanc. (Dubbeljoint was a cross-border company touring throughout Ireland deriving its name from DUBlin and BELfast.) Dubbeljoint was founded to present work that reflected the political climate in Northern Ireland and to be a borderless company which could perform between the North and South of Ireland. Early works for Dubbeljoint included: *Hang All the Harpers* (1991), Belfast Christmas tale *Christmas Eve Can Kill You* (1991), and Gogol's classic comedy *The Government Inspector* (1993) adapted by Jones, which was celebrated by critics across the United

Kingdom and Ireland. In 1994 the play transferred to the Tricycle in London.

The Government Inspector was written by Gogol in 1834 as a satire on the corrupt, oppressive bureaucrats of Tsarist Russia. When Jones decided to adapt Gogol's comedy she substituted late-19th century Ireland for mid-19th century Russia. She replaced a group of provincial Russians, and their desire to mimic Moscow, with their counterparts in Northern Ireland, who believed in the superiority of a British accent. Jones set the play at the end of the nineteenth-century when Ireland was governed by Westminster. Despite the huge momentum for Home Rule, the idea of Partition had begun to be whispered, as a temporary solution, to keep a portion of Ireland within the United Kingdom.

In Jones' adaptation the Tsarist backwater becomes an outpost of Protestant ascendancy where Catholic peasants replace serfs and Westminster replaces Moscow. The play was "armed with that historical supergun, and scabrously brilliant dialogue suggesting Somerville and Ross done over by Brendan Behan ... a detailed farcical energy the like of which I have not seen since Jean Meyer at the Comédie-Française". (Wardle, 1994)

A Night in November (1998) was Jones' second major work for Dubbeljoint Productions and was first performed at the West Belfast Festival at Whiterock. The play was Jones' most successful for Dubbeljoint, winning several prestigious awards and further performances in London and New York. There were extensive tours in Northern Ireland and three times to the Irish Republic with a five week run at Eamonn Doran's Bar in Dublin and seven weeks at the Andrews Lane Theatre in Dublin. This was followed by a five week run at the Tricycle Theatre in London and two weeks at Sidetracks in New York City.

A Night in November was provoked, rather than inspired, by the happenings at the Northern Ireland v Republic of Ireland World Cup qualifying match in Windsor Park, Belfast, November 1993. The intensity of sectarian bigotry and hatred, expressed at the match, so soon after the murders in the village of Greysteel, shocked many people north and south of the border. As Jack Charlton's Republic of Ireland team came on to the pitch, they were greeted with chants of "Greysteel, Greysteel. Greysteel seven, Ireland nil" and "Trick or Treat?" The heckling referenced Northern Ireland's most recent massacre when loyalist gunmen entered a bar in the predominantly Catholic village of Greysteel in County Derry. Before opening fire, the gunmen had shouted a Halloween chorus of "Trick or Treat?" The gunmen left seven people dead and more than twenty wounded. The events at Windsor Park that evening prompted Jones to write *A Night in November*.

Kenneth McAllister, from a lower middle-class Protestant family, is increasingly uneasy about his identity and his place in Northern Ireland that he always assumed was created for a Protestant population. Kenneth, like most in his community, kept his head down, looked after his own business and did not shoot Catholics. He believed, along with the loyalist killers, in his Protestant ascendancy rights; he deplored the killings, but did nothing to change his views on sectarianism.

Kenneth is a Social Security clerk living a humdrum life in Belfast, tolerating his marriage and his in-laws, until the fateful night in November when he begins his rebellious journey from Belfast's Windsor Park to Doran's Bar in New York. As he crosses the tarmac at Dublin airport he looks back at his whole predictable existence, roars with laughter, and boards the Aer Lingus flight to New York. Kenneth realises that, but for "moving away to respectability and a couple of exams and a job" he could also have been like his boyhood friend, Norman, who was killed while planting a bomb intended for Catholics: "We were civilised so we closed our eyes and our Venetians and let Norman Dawson ... we let Norman Dawson do it for us. Oh, yes, we showed our disgust, tutted loudly and then scurried back in to the ten-by-ten and never thought of Norman Dawson or his victims ever again" (27). *A Night in November* is a compelling, ecstatic, two-hour monologue about how an ordinary Department of Health and Social Security clerk, who is Protestant, uptight, middle-class and a bigot, begins to turn away from the tribal politics of his people and to discover his new identity as a Protestant Irishman. The play is a confrontation with the cultural reality of the Catholic-Protestant divide in Northern Ireland.

Kenneth's road to Damascus began when he brought his bigoted father-in-law to watch the infamous football game at Windsor Park and to New York. In New York he found himself with the football supporters who had witnessed Ireland's brief triumph over Italy in the World Cup. There could hardly have been a "more appropriate time (the age of the peace process) or a more appropriate space (the bar-room basement of Eamonn Doran's new bar-restaurant in Crown Alley Dublin. This ambience is transposed to his New York establishment which has been a home-from-home for Irish transients of all persuasions on Second Avenue) for the staging in Dublin of Dubbeljoint's brilliant presentation of Marie Jones' sharp edged, soft-centred presentation of the conversion of Kenneth McAllister from acquiescent and unquestioning Protestant dole clerk to ardent member of Jack's army." (Nowland, 1994)

Kenneth portrays an array of characters in the monologue: venomous father-in-law, complacent housebound wife, neighbours and crowds of drunken soccer supporters whom he joins on his trip to New York. Jones found a way to write an angry, funny and compassionate one-man play that confronts the bigotry in Ulster Protestantism that revealed itself that night at the Windsor Park football stadium. The success of the play in Ireland has been Jones' willingness to say what, until this time, had gone unsaid and, like Sam Thompson, being a member of the 'tribe', she could say it. It is easy to condemn the sectarian killings but the play focuses on a more elusive phenomenon, the genteel discrimination of the Belfast middle classes. In Kenneth McAllister's world, Catholics have always been despised and judged: " ... bikes and the scooters scattered over the lawn meant slovenliness, a pile of jumbled books meant no pride or dignity in their lives, a wife who said cook your own tea meant low life at its lowest and all this meant second class, filth, scum and hatred ... and I believed it." (26)

Kenneth's wife, Debrah, sees herself and her family as ordered "perfect Prods": "She will make herself believe with the same will and determination that she does her step-ups in aerobics, with the same rigour that she cleans the house, the same dedication she puts into making sure the kids are going to pass the eleven-plus, the same willpower she has for sacrifice to better herself because it's all part of the same thing ... all part of the same thing ... We are the perfect Prods, we come in kits, we are standard regulation, we come from one design, like those standard kitchens with exact spaces for standard cookers and fridges, our dimensions never vary and that's the way we want it, but what happens when the kit is put together and the appliances don't fit the spaces ... what happens ... chaos, mayhem and we can't cope, we can't cope."(23) Jones, a dismantler of female stereotypes, creates one of the most horrific stereotypes in Kenneth's wife.

The price of Kenneth's sense of superiority is alienation in Protestant Northern Ireland where he is neither wholly British or Irish. Kenneth's emotional and political journey removes him from the narrow Northern Irish perspectives towards a more tolerant world. In New York he realises that he can lose the fear and prejudice that has governed his life, with the acceptance that he can be both Protestant and Irish at the same time. *A Night in November* questions the unquestionable in Protestant culture.

Underneath the farce and slapstick humour is a deeply nuanced and instinctive understanding of human behaviour that surfaces to raise consistent and provocative questions about the Ulster Protestant. The first half of the play overplays the Protestant ethos, cleanliness is next to godliness, and the bigotry of petty suburban Protestant snobbery stands in stark contrast to the dishevelled joys of being Catholic. As Kenneth becomes more enlightened, he tries to escape the inertia and self-satisfied bourgeois life in a Belfast suburb. Jones leaves us feeling great compassion for Kenneth as he struggles to overcome his upbringing and life-long prejudice towards the Catholic population. Jones' compassionate portrayal of Kenneth in *A Night in November* resolves into a glimmer of hope for the future of Northern Ireland.

Stones in His Pockets has been Jones' most successful play. It has been performed in many major cities around the world including London and New York. *Stones in His Pockets* toured Ireland in 1996 with a four-week run at Dublin's Tivioli Theatre, during the Dublin Theatre Festival. It opened at the Lyric Theatre, Belfast in June 1999 before a short run at the Belfast Opera House. Further performances at the Tricycle Theatre, London, extended to thirteen weeks. A West End management booked the play for the New Ambassador Theatre and with continuing success to an unlimited run at the Duke of York's in London. Jones received many awards during the London performances: the 2001 Olivier Award for Best Comedy, *Irish Post* Award for Literature (2000), *Irish Times* Irish Theatre Award for Best Production (1999), the *Evening Standard* Award in London as Best Comedy (2000).

Stones in His Pockets follows the lives of two men, Jake and Charlie, both in their thirties, aimless and unemployed. They fantasise about becoming film stars during their work as extras on an American movie, *The Quiet Valley*, being filmed on Ireland's west coast. The play explores the hopes and ideas of how the future should look through the comic evaluation of the film industry in Ireland and its impact on Jake, Charlie and Irish culture in general. Jake and Charlie impersonate many characters including: the female star of the movie, the director, the production assistant and various locals working on the movie that is set in County Kerry.

Jake and Charlie are happy to earn "forty quid a day ...

rubbing shoulders with the stars." The story of the movie, *The Quiet Valley*, is a preposterous only-in-Hollywood version of Ireland. A young woman, from the landed gentry, falls in love with a peasant who marries her and proceeds to give the land back to the people. Jake demonstrates for Charlie what they are supposed to do in one of the extras scenes as he hunches over and puts on a plaintive expression, deftly transforming himself into a beaten-down supplicant. He knows that he and all the other extras are simply background, like the landscape itself, the Blasket Islands in the distance.

The 'Stones' of the title refer to a suicidal drowning and, metaphorically, to the oppression of an impoverished rural people fed on unrealisable dreams. The death of the young village drug addict highlights the deceptions and distortions of Hollywood plots, especially when the budget-conscious Americans are insensitive about the funeral that they dismiss as a professional inconvenience. The play clearly highlights the demise of many of Ireland's rural communities as Jones exploits the irony of exploited Irishmen playing dispossessed, nineteenth-century Irish peasants.

The rural Ireland of Jones' imagination is not the blighted and benighted place we've come to know from Martin McDonagh's *Leenane Trilogy*: "This Ireland is somewhat more benign, not rotten at the core but a blinkered victim of bad luck and foreign—and in this case, American—exploitation." (Franklin, 2001) Jones has been compared to other, successful, international Irish playwrights: "So do we fall to our knees before yet another messiah of a dramatist? Is Ms. Jones the new Conor McPherson, who was said to be the new Martin McDonagh, who was said to be the new Brian Friel ... Well, let's stop there. It is undeniable that without Ireland western theatre today would be much the poorer. And Ms. Jones makes her own distinctive contribution to the fine art of theatrical storytelling ... But it should be noted that the pleasures of *Stones in His Pockets* are less literary than kinetic." (Brantley, 2001)

Stones in His Pockets is a tour de force for both actors and demands great physicality in the swift changes between the many characters. Jones has also expressed her amazement at what the actors and director did with her simple stage direction (they dance): "and what they do is incredible. It's brilliant to watch, I can't believe they've done this. It's the nuances they create. Ian McElhinney, the director for the London and New York performances, spent hours and hours on the script and the staging is simple with beautiful effects." (Love, 24)

Jones has been producing new plays at an astounding rate during the past seventeen years. As an actress, Jones has performed in most theatres in Ireland with many touring Irish theatre companies and toured internationally in many of her own productions. For BBC Radio Four she has played in numerous productions: from Natasha in Brian Friel's adaptation of *The Three Sisters* to a cow in Gerry Stembridge's *Daisy the Cow Who Talked*. She has appeared in many television dramas and in film, including the role of Sarah Conlon in *In the Name of the Father*.

Jones, like Thompson and Parker, believes that east Belfast has been important for her creative process as it is what informs her work: "It is what I am. My background is important to me. It might take a month to write a play. That's the physical act. In reality it has taken me all my life. Nearly every time I've known who I was writing for. It's very focused. It frees you to do what you want. It makes the plays more vivid. And I enjoy the relationship with actors." (Love, 24)

Jones has become a significant Irish playwright and holds a mirror up to Northern Irish society. In a country where men's images of men, and men's images of women dominate the stage, a play written by a woman is regularly criticised or rejected for not complying to these norms. The lack of appreciation for women's work could be seen in subtly anti-feminist reviews in some Irish newspapers. Jones had learned from her early years in the theatre and particularly her work for ten years with

Charabanc that she needed to be audacious and to show women, in all of their complexity, on stage: "Although it is not surprising that female playwrights present a different view of Irish womanhood than do male playwrights, what is most telling is how female writers recast the stereotypes; gone is the depiction of women as either unattainable saints or bewitching sinners; gone is the mystery surrounding their behaviour." (Harris, 115) Jones is one of the few Irish female playwrights to be produced internationally and is a significant playwright by any standard. She continues to explore new and innovative work that is rooted in Ireland but is not inhibited or restricted by its geographical territory.

CONCLUSION

The cultural heritage of the Ulster Protestant is on shifting ground as past identification with England and hostility towards the Irish Republic has led to an acute identity crisis. This crisis was reflected in Northern Irish drama after 1960 beginning with Sam Thompson's *Over the Bridge*. Many of the themes and obsessions that dominated the theatre in Ulster after 1960 show the dramatist moving away from the archaic signs in the Ulster landscape towards a more inclusive society.

Northern Irish drama has had a distinctive tradition that is separate, in important ways, from the celebrated drama of the Irish Republic and the Abbey tradition. Northern Irish theatre has often been a minor inclusion in critical works that surveyed Irish theatre. In Declan Kiberd's critical study, *Inventing Ireland* (1995), Stewart Parker, undoubtedly a major playwright, is not mentioned. Christopher Fitz-Simon in his survey, *The Irish Theatre* (1994), devotes less than one page to Northern Irish drama and includes four playwrights in part of his chapter 'Irish Drama Outside Dublin', mentioning only Sam Thompson, John Boyd, Patrick Galvin and Martin Lynch. D.E.S. Maxwell in *A Critical Study of Modern Irish Drama* (1984) devotes nine pages to Northern Irish dramatists including: Sam Thompson, John Boyd,

Wilson John Haire, Tom MacIntyre, Bill Morrison, Stewart Parker, Graham Reid and Brian Friel. By contrast, Anthony Roche in *Contemporary Irish Drama, from Beckett to McGuinness* (1995), and Christopher Murray's *Twentieth Century Irish Drama: Mirror Up to Nature* (1997) devote substantial chapters to the drama of Northern Ireland.

Thompson's work was prophetic as it foreshadowed a community that, sooner or later, was doomed to another violent and bloody period in its history. Playwrights have played an important role in reflecting these events. Northern Irish drama has come to command more critical attention in the past twenty years, not only in the work of Marie Jones and Gary Mitchell, but also Christina Reid, Anne Devlin, Martin Lynch and Graham Reid, all of whom came to public attention in the 1980s and 1990s. This flowering of dramatic activity (even as the sectarian conflict dragged on) deserves attention as a phenomenon separate, to some degree, from Irish Drama in general.

Northern Ireland has entered into a relatively peaceful period of co-existence between rival religious factions in recent years. Much has been written about the increasing degree of alienation in the Protestant community resulting from years of discrimination against the Catholic community and the present attempts to redress that balance. The Protestant community has felt threatened by the Peace Agreement that it sees as too conciliatory towards Nationalist aims. Protestants are trying to emphasise their own culture in an attempt to forge their Northern Irish identity.

Symbols, as manifestations of cultural identity, are important in Northern Ireland and the Unionist tradition experienced freedom to display and proclaim its cultural symbols. The Nationalist community was prevented from doing likewise by the many legal restrictions that had been put in place by successive Unionist governments. The more obvious manifestations of cultural life in Northern Ireland are inextricably built into the separated communities. Playwrights have tried to find a context in which the shared hatred between Catholic and Protestant could be reconciled. The plays that register aspects of the social and political life reveal the writers as 'the antennae of the race' as the playwrights confront society, not because it is fashionable, but because of the artist's instinct that he or she should do so.

The four playwrights represented in this book are all Protestant—that is, they write from within the majority community in Northern Ireland, though none is in any sense an apologist for that community; the four adopt attitudes towards Northern Irish Protestant culture that range from the angrily condemnatory (Thompson) to the gently satirical (Jones). Some Northern Irish Catholic playwrights who have given valuable dramatic insights to Northern Irish Protestantism might easily have been included, most notably Brian Friel (especially *The Freedom of the City*). Sam Thompson, Stewart Parker, Gary Mitchell and Marie Jones, along with their fellow Protestant playwrights, form a coherent group that can be considered separately, as well as within a broader context (in a different work).

The playwrights break into two pairs, beginning in 1960: a first generation and a second. Thompson's *Over the Bridge* is included for its historic interest as the first modern play that attempted a frank exposé of Northern Irish sectarianism. Back in the 1960s there were hopes that Northern Ireland might produce a theatre that would look at its own troubles. Thompson's work for the stage was written in the vernacular and portrayed the day-to-day sectarian bitterness, in the city's then great shipyards, as a searing indictment of the North's divided society. This was coupled with the cynicism of politicians and big business that profited by exploiting those divides and diverted attention from other social problems. Thompson tried to break the barriers of bigotry in his attempts to create a theatre that could function independently of Unionist hegemony. *Over the*

Bridge was a foundational event in the creation of modern Northern Irish drama because Thompson dared to address the subject of sectarianism directly and thus opened the Northern Irish theatre to a new kind of honesty and a new willingness to address Northern Irish conditions critically.

The political theatre that had disappeared for almost forty years, since O'Casey's Dublin trilogy, came back with vengeance in Thompson's work. Before Thompson there were plays that startled the bourgeoisie for a week or so and then disappeared. Thompson's work did not disappear, as was hoped, his plays looked head-on at Ulster society and served as a model for other northern playwrights, particularly in the work of Gary Mitchell.

Many dramatists north and south of the border had staged the Troubles, often in the Protestant satirical tradition of Oliver Goldsmith and Oscar Wilde, while others approached the subject matter through a more literary and romantic Catholic tradition. Writers in Northern Ireland had the ability to write with humour and fantasy using local dialect and satire in a way that allowed them to present tragic circumstances in an entertaining way. Stewart Parker carried on Thompson's work in a long series of plays that attempted to address the same issues but with very different theatrical means.

Parker's work is in the satirical tradition but often his whimsical style and his love of wordplay distracted the critics from the power of his work, which is often a threnody for Belfast, a city he loved, and one which was being slowly destroyed by the IRA and the city planners. Parker's work gives an image of hope, in what seemed a hopeless situation, as he worked in an atmosphere of despair which was, for many, the most common response to the violence in Northern Ireland. Ulster Protestantism harbours many trappings and tribal attitudes that Parker tried to unravel, to find a history of the Protestant culture that is enabling, rather than one which is inward looking and static. Thompson's grim naturalism is replaced in Parker's plays by a playful meta-dramatic style that culminates in his *Three Plays for Ireland* which use fantasy and comedy to explore topics that Thompson had addressed with angry, deliberately provocative realism.

The Northern Protestant dramatist has been forced to re-examine the outworn myths of the past and to point a way forward which is inclusive and creates a tolerable order in society. The uncertainties that exist in the Protestant North are reflected most recently in the work of Gary Mitchell in which he explores the complexities of Protestant culture that leave no room for illusory or indulgent images of that community. Mitchell writes in the tough vernacular of the North and, like Thompson, he is a proletarian playwright. His plays are not of social protest but brutal family plays in which the crisis facing the working-class Protestant after the Peace Agreement, and the ambiguity of Protestant culture, are explored.

Marie Jones' theatrical landscape has been expansive over the past seventeen years and her plays highlight the problems that face contemporary society through an acute observation of life in Northern Ireland. The recent success of *Stones in His Pockets* may have overshadowed much of her early work that has been important for the development of women writers in Northern Ireland. Jones has examined Northern Irish culture in her plays as she has stripped away stereotypes and exposed the fears and prejudices of both communities in Northern Ireland. Jones' plays are more than a mere reflection of life, they are socially committed, and in the tradition of Thompson and Parker, they illuminate a path forward.

Works Cited

Allen, Robert. 'Playwright from a Lost Tribe'. *Irish Times* 31 January 1987.

Andrews, Elmer. 'The Power of Play'. *Theatre Ireland* 18 (April-June 1989): 21-28.

——. 'The Will to Freedom'. *Theatre Ireland* 19 (July-September 1989): 19-23.

BBC Radio Northern Ireland Archives. 'The Making of a Musical'. 1 February 1978.

Bell, Sam Hanna. *The Theatre in Ulster*. Dublin: Gill and Macmillan, 1972.

Billington, Michael. '*Kingdom Come*'. *Guardian* 18 January 1978.

——. '*Catchpenny Twist*'. *Guardian* 22 February 1980.

——. 'Hope in *Heartbreak House*'. *Guardian* 11 January 1989.

——. 'Summer and the rioting is easy'. *Guardian* 17 June, 2000.

Boland, Lar. *Irish Tribune Magazine* 16 February 1997.

Bradley, Lara. 'Taking the traditional route ... ' *Belfast News Letter-City Limits* 17 June, 2000.

Brantley, Ben. 'Wearing Everyone's Shoes, Yet Being Themselves'. *New York Times* 2 April 2001.

Brighton, Pam. 'Charabanc'. *Theatre Ireland*. (September-December 1990): 41.

Brown, Terence. 'History's Nightmare: Stewart Parker's *Northern Star*'. *Theatre Ireland* 13 (1987): 40-41.

Byrne, Ophelia. *The Stage in Ulster from the Eighteenth Century*. Belfast: The Linen Hall Library. 1997.

Carty, Ciaran. '*Northern Star* Rising on the Tide'. *Irish Sunday Tribune* 29 September 1985.

Chrisafis, Angelique. 'Loyalist paramilitaries drive playwright from his home'. *Guardian Unlimited* 21 September 2005.

Clarke, Joycelyn. 'First Nights'. *Irish Sunday Tribune* 22 March 1998.

Cooper, Robert. 'Riveting Exchanges: Stewart Parker'. Supplement to *Fortnight* 298 (November 1989): 5.

Coyle, Jane. 'Charabanc in Top Gear'. *Irish News* 10 August 1984.

——. 'Mapping the Hard Road'. *Irish Times* 8 February 1997.

——. 'Big World of His Own'. *The Stage* 26 February 1998.

Cushman, Robert. 'Belfast Songsters'. *Observer* 24 February 1980.

Darby, John. *Scorpions in a Bottle*. London: Minority Rights Publications. 1997.

Deane, Seamus. Programme notes for *Northern Star*. Tinderbox Theatre Company 1998.

Devlin, Paddy. 'An Author Who Crossed the Bridge'. *Belfast News Letter* 25 July 1985.

Dewhurst, Keith. 'Uniting Irishmen'. *Guardian* 5 November 1988.

DiCenzo, Maria. 'Charabanc Theatre Company: Placing Women Centre Stage in Northern Ireland'. *Theatre Journal* (45) 1993.

Eder, Richard. 'Spokesong: Belfast Drama at Long Wharf'. *New York Times* 11 February 1978.

Ervine, David. 'Making a point with a play'. *Belfast News Letter-City Limits* 17 June 2000.

Farrell, Michael. *Northern Ireland: The Orange State*. London: Pluto Press. 2nd. Ed. 1980.

Foster, Roy. The Magazine-Ireland. 19 May 1998.

Franklin, Nancy. 'Blarney Stones'. *New Yorker* 16 April 2001.

Fricker, Karen. 'A World Apart'. *American Theater* 19 May 1998.

Grant, David. *The Crack in the Emerald*. London: Nick Hern Books. 2nd. Ed., 1990.

Harris, Claudia. 'From Pastness to Wholeness: Stewart Parker's Reinventing Theatre'. *Colby Quarterly* 27.4 (December 1991): 233-41.

——. Biographical notes on Stewart Parker.

——. The State of Play: Irish Theatre in the Nineties.Trier: Wissenschaftlicher Verlag. 1996 pp. 104-124.

Heaney, Mick. 'Spotlight turns to orange'. *Sunday Times* 11 June, 2000.

Heaney, Seamus. 'Victorious Ulsterman'. *Sunday Independent* (Ireland) 6 November 1988.

Jones, Marie. A draft copy of an interview with Charabanc by Carol Martin for publication in the *Drama Review*. 8 November 1986.

——. *A Night in November*. London: Nick Hern Books, 1995.

——. *The Hamster Wheel*. London:Nick Hern Books, 1990.

Kennedy, Douglas. Programme notes to Rough Magic production of *Nightshade* 1987.

Keyes, John. Introduction to *Over the Bridge and Other Plays* Belfast: Lagan Press 1997.

Killen, John. 'Rutherford Mayne, Selected Plays'. Belfast: Institute of Irish Studies. Queen's University Belfast, 1997

Kilroy, Thomas. Programme notes for *Northern Star*. Tinderbox Theatre Company 1998.

Kinsella, Thomas. *The Tain*. Oxford: Oxford University Press. 1969.

Lojak, Helen. 'Playing Politics with Belfast's Charabanc Theatre Company'. *Politics and Performance In Contemporary Northern Ireland*. Amhurst: University of Mass. Press. American Conference for Irish Studies. 1999.

Longley, Edna. 'The Writer and Belfast': *The Irish Writer and the City: Irish Literary Studies* 18 ed. Maurice Harmon. St Gerrards Cross: Colin Smythe 1984.

Love, Walter. 'Marie Jones, Actress and Playwright'. *Ulster Tatler* October 2000: 23-24.

Lyons, Laura. 'Of Orangemen and Green Theatres'. *A Century of Irish Drama*. Bloomington: Indiana University Press, 2000.

Magee, John. *Northern Ireland: Crisis and Conflict*. London: Routledge, 1974.

Maxwell, D.E.S. *Modern Irish Drama 1891-1989*. Cambridge: Cambridge University Press, 1984.

McCann, Eamon, Programme notes for *As the Beast Sleeps*. The Peacock Theatre, Dublin 1998.

McCracken, Kathleen. 'Fractures and Continuities: Melodramatic Elements in Stewart Parker's *Nightshade*'. *Notes on Modern Irish Literature* 2 (1990): 68-73.

McFadden, Grania. 'Menacing tale low on drama'. *Belfast Telegraph* 18 March 1998.

——. 'Mitchell's marching season lacks edge and menace'. *Belfast Telegraph* 14 June, 2000.

McGuinness, Frank. 'Stewart Parker'. *Independent* 5 November 1989.

Mengel, Hagal. *Sam Thompson and Modern Drama in Ulster*. New York: Peter Lang. 1986.

Mitchell, Gary. *Tearing the Loom* and *In a Litttle World of Our Own*. London: Nick Hern Books, 1998.

——. *Trust*. London: Nick Hern Books, 1999.

Mooney, Cathy, 'A Small Question of Identity'. *Irish News* 10 October 1997.

Moore, Carol. *Sunday World*-Ireland 12 October 1997.

Murray, Christopher. *Twentieth Century Irish Drama: Mirror Up To Nation*. Manchester: University Press, 1997.

Nowland, David. '*A Night in Novemeber* ... Eamon Doran's Imbibing Emporium'. *Irish Times* 11 November 1994.

——. 'Compelling dissection of human conflict'. *Irish Times* 11 June 1998.

——. '*Somewhere Over the Balcony* at the Peacock'. 19 December 1987.

——. '*Pratt's Fall* at The Eblana'. *Irish Times* 27 September 1983.

O'Brian, Conor C. 'A Song of Disbafflement'. *Observer* 29 January 1978.

O'Kelly, Emer. 'A World Falling Apart'. *Irish Sunday Independent* 14 June, 1998.

O'Toole, Fintan. 'Unsung Heroines Take a Bow'. *Irish Times* 2 June, 1990.

——. 'Doomed Dreams of Decency'. *Irish Times* 18 February 1997.

——. 'Death and Resurrection'. *Irish Sunday Times* 27 September 1987.

Parker, Stewart:

——. 1977 Programme notes for *Catchpenny Twist*.

——. 1978 *Kingdom Come*. Unpublished script. The Stewart Parker Collection. Linen Hall Library, Belfast.

——. 'State of Play'. *Canadian Journal of Irish Studies*. 7.1 (June 1981): 5-11.

——. 'Me and Jim'. *Irish University Review: A Journal of Irish Studies* 12.1 (Spring 1982): 32-34.

——. 1984 Programme notes for *Northern Star*.

——.'Signpost'. *Theatre Ireland*.11 (Nov-December 1985): 27-29

——. 'Dramatis Personae'. John Malone Memorial Lecture. Belfast: Queen's University, 1986.

——. 1987 *Lost Belongings*. Unpublished script. The Stewart Parker

Collection. Linen Hall Library, Belfast.

——. 1989 *Three Plays for Ireland*. London: Oberon Books, 1989.

——. *Stewart Parker: Plays 1* London: Methuen Publishing Limited, 2000.

——. *Stewart Parker: Plays 2* London: Methuen Publishing Limited, 2000.

Parkin, Andrew. 'Metaphor as Dramatic Structure in Three Plays by Stewart Parker'. *Irish Writers and the Theatre*. Ed., Masaru Sekine. Gerrards Cross: Colin Smythe, 1986. 135-150.

Peter, John. 'Innocents in an Irish Minefield'. *Sunday Times* 2 March 1980.

Smith, John. 'Piercing, Patient Observation'. *Fortnight*. Belfast, November 1996.

Smyth, Damian. *Martin Lynch: Three Plays*. Belfast: Lagan Press, 1996.

Sullivan, Megan. *Women in Northern Ireland*. University Press of Florida. 1999.

Taylor, Paul. 'On the Treadmill'. *Independent* 4 May, 1990.

Thompson, Sam. Collection held at the Belfast Central Library. Contains 16 filling Boxes divided into 12 sections: documentary records, scripts, letters, photos and other memorabilia.

Wardle, Irving. 'The skull beneath the farce'. *Independent on Sunday* 6 February 1994.

Whelan, Kevin. Programme notes for *Northern Star*. Tinderbox Theatre Company 1998.

Willet, John. *The Theatre of Erwin Piscator*. London: Eyre Methuen. 1978.

Williams, Caroline. 'Who is Keeping Irish Women out of the Mainstream'. *Theatre Ireland* 6, 1993.

Yeats, W.B., *Samhain*, published Irish Literary Theatre. 1901-06, six issues; 1908, one issue.

Index

Abbey Theatre 21, 26, 62, 63, 162
Abrams, M.H 13-14
Abyssinia
  invaded by Italy 33
Act of Union 73
Aeschylus 65
Albee, Edward 48
Alliance Party 147
Ammons, A.R. 54
Andrews, Elmer 99, 110
Andrews, Thomas 71, 73
Andrews Lane Theatre, Dublin 197
Anglo-Irish Agreement 116
Anglo-Irish theatre 128
Ardhowen theatre, Enniskillen 191
Artauds, Antonin 64
Arts Council of Northern Ireland 75, 76, 193
Arts Theatre, Belfast 190, 191, 194
Ashfield School 51
Auden, W.H. 69-70, 94

Ballyhackamore 51
Baraka, Amiri 16
  Dutchmen (1964) 16
  Slave Ship (1969) 16
BBC, Belfast 32, 42, 43, 56, 57, 75
  see also Heffernan, Michael;
  McKee, Ritchie; Thompson, Sam
  'Play For Today' 89
  The Island Men 32
Beckett, Samuel 62, 119, 126, 127, 135, 154
  Waiting for Godot 62, 130
Behan, Brendan 63, 127, 135, 197
  The Hostage 55
Belfast Arts Award for Television 159
Belfast Arts Drama Award 160
Belfast Band Scene 89
Belfast Blitz 82
Belfast Empire Theatre 44
Belfast Festival Poets series 53
Belfast Harp Festival 127, 133

Belfast Linen Mills 189
Belfast News Letter 134
Belfast Opera House 201
Belfast Variety Markets 190
Belfast Youth Theatre 161, 185
Belvoir Players 188
Billington, Michael 105
Bishop, Elizabeth 185
Blakely, Colin 43
Blaeu, William
  'The Light of Navigation' 112
Bloody Friday 82
Bloody Sunday 82
Boucicault, Dion 120, 127, 128, 132, 136-45
  London Assurance 138, 142
  The Colleen Bawn (1860) 138
  The Indian Mutiny 143
  The Jilt 144
  The Octoroon 143-4
  The Shaughran 145
Boyd, John 205
Boyd, Stephen 43
Brecht, Bertolt 16, 35, 58-61, 67, 94, 193
  'On Experimental Theatre' (1939) 60
  Small Organum for the Theatre (1948) 60
  Baal 59
  Lehrstücke 58
Brechtian theatre 85
Brighton, Pam 162, 190, 191, 196
British Rail 76
Brookeborough, Lord 41, 44

Carnduff, Thomas 41
  Songs from the Shipyard (1924) 41
  Workers (1932) 41
Casement Prize (1933-34) 27
Castlereagh Road 33
Catholic Standard 42
Cave Hill 129
Celtic Mysticism 22
Chamberlain, Lord 42

Charabanc Theatre Company 18, 46, 183, 185, 186, 188, 189-91, 193-4, 196, 204
Charles Wintor Award 160
Charlton, Jack 198
Church of Ireland Gazette 42
Churchill, Randolph 81
Civil Rights movement (USA) 16
Clarence Place Hall 24
Clarence Players 188
Columbus, Christopher 100, 111
Congreve, William 110, 143
Connolly, James 189
Convent Garden Theatre 141
Cornell University 54, 119
Corrymeela Community 90
Cosgrave, Liam 147
Council for the Encouragement of Music and Arts 44
Cousins, James 23
  The Racing Lug 23
Craig, James 150
Craigmore Street 33
Cruise O'Brien, Conor 104
Cushman, Robert 95

D'Arcy, Margaret 43
Davey, Shaun 89, 95, 96, 100, 102, 105
Deane, Seamus 52, 121
Deirdre of the Sorrows 114
Devlin, Anne 206
Devlin, J.G. 43
Disraeli, Benjamin 138
Donmar Warehouse, London 168
Drill Hall, London 191-2
Drumcree March 180
Dubbeljoint Productions 196-7
Dublin High Court 41
Dublin Theatre Festival 42, 45, 46, 57, 74, 76, 191, 201
Duke of York, London 201
Dunlop, John 63, 78, 81
Dunlop Tyre Company 76

Eamonn Doran's Bar, Dublin 197
Edinburgh Festival Fringe 75, 191

Edwards, Hilton 45
Edwards-MacLiammoir Productions 46
Elbow Rooms 46
Elliman, Louis 44
Ellis, James 43, 44, 46, 76
Ellman, Richard 68
English Stage Company 179
Ervine, David 181
Ervine, St John 41
  Mixed Marriage (1911) 41
Euripides 65
Eurovision Song Contest 95, 96, 99
Evening Standard Award 201
Everyman 35, 51-2

Farquhar, George 110, 119, 126, 127, 128, 142
  The Recruiting Officer 142
Faulkner, Brian 147, 148
Field Day Theatre Company 146
Fitt, Gerry 147
Fitz-Simon, Christopher 205
  The Irish Theatre 205
French Revolution 124
Friel, Brian 202, 203, 206
  Francophile (1959) 43
  The Freedom of the City 207

Galvin, Patrick 205
Garrett, Brian 76
George Devine Award 160
German Expressionist theatre 69
Gibson, Catherine 43
Gibson, Harry S. 27
  Bannister's Café (1949) 27
  The Square Peg (1950) 27
Gillespie, Robert 89
Gogol, Nikolai 197
  The Government Inspector (1834) 197
Goldblatt, Harold 43
Goldsmith, Oliver 110, 128, 142, 208
  She Stoops to Conquer 130, 142
  The Good Natured Man 130
Gonne, Maud 23, 82
Grand Opera House, Belfast 45

Grant, David
  Playing the Wild Card 194
Great War see World War I
Gregory, Lady 63
Greysteel massacre 198
Grotowoskis, Jerzy 64
Group Theatre 43, 44
Guardian, the 105
Guildhall, Londonderry 145-6

Haire, Wilson John 206
Hamlet 13
Hamilton College, Utica 54
Hanna Bell, Sam 27, 32
Harland & Wolff 15, 31, 32, 33, 54, 69
Hartford Stage Company, USA 89
Heaney, Seamus 52, 53, 54, 156
Heath, Ted 147
Heffernan, Michael 57-8, 75-6
Hepburn, Doreen 43
Hindemith, Paul 59
Hinds, Andy 190
Hobsbaum, Philip 53
Hobson, Bulmer 23
  Brian of Bamba (1904) 24
Home Movement Reformists 24
Home Rule Bills 81
Huizinga, Johan 16, 64, 112
  Homo Ludens 64
Hume, John 155

Ibsen, Henrik 15, 22
In the Name of the Father 203
International Theatre Festival 191
Irish Republican Army (IRA) 104,
  105, 147
'Irish Drama' 63
Irish Home Rule Bill 69
Irish Independence 22
Irish Land Commission 27
Irish Literary Theatre 23
Irish Post Award 201
Irish Revival 111
Irish Theatre Awards 160, 162
Irish Times 26, 55, 56
Irish Times Best Production Award
  160, 201

Isherwood, Christopher 69, 94
Ixion Productions 75-6

John Player Theatre, Dublin 74
Johnston, Dennis 47
Jones, Marie 14, 18, 47, 183-204, 206,
  207
  A Night in November (1998) 18, 197-
201
  Christmas Eve Can Kill You (1991)
196
  Hang All the Harpers (1991) 196
  Lay Up Your Ends (1983) 18, 46,
189-91
  Now You're Talking (1985) 191
  Oul Delf and False Teeth (1984) 190-1
  Ruby (2000) 186
  Somewhere Over the Balcony (1987)
18, 191-3
  Stones in His Pockets 18, 201-3, 209
  The Girls in the Big Picture (1986)
191, 194
  The Government Inspector (1993)
196-7
  The Hamster Wheel (1990) 18, 186,
194-6
  Women on the Verge of HRT (1996)
186
Joyce, James 55, 56-7, 62, 64, 68, 120,
128
  *A Portrait of the Artist as a Young
Man* 56, 68, 120
  Dubliners 68
  Ulysses 42, 68, 128

Kane, Whitford (1881-1956) 25-6
Keane, Charles 138, 145
Kelly, Billy 149
Kibert, Declan
  Inventing Ireland 205
Killanin, Lord 45
King James 25, 121
King Louis 123
King William of Orange 15, 25
King's Head Theatre, London 77,
  89, 100

Laffan, Patrick 89
Lardner, Dr Dionysius 137, 140
Lewis, Irene 89
Littlewoods Department Store 187
Littlewoods, Joan 64
Long Wharf Theatre, New Haven 77
Longley, Edna 69
 'The Writer and Belfast' 69
Longley, Michael 52
'Lost Tribe' 13, 14, 47, 157
'Ludic Theatre' 64
Luke, Peter 45
Lynch, Martin 189-90, 205, 206
Lyric Youth Theatre 187
Lyric Theatre, Belfast 75, 119, 162-3, 175, 180, 183, 185, 187, 188, 201

Mac Anna, Tómas 45
MacNamara, Gerald 15, 47
 see also Morrow, Harry C.
 Suzanne and the Sovereigns (1907) 15, 25
MacIntyre, Tom 206
Madison Square Theatre, New York 136
Mahon, Derek 52
Malone, John 51-2, 64
Matthews, Charles 141
Mason, Patrick 146
Maxwell, D.E.S. 94
 A Critical Study of Modern Irish Drama (1984) 205-6
Mayne, Rutherford,
 see Waddell, Sam
 Bridgehead (1934) 26, 27
 Peter (1930) 26
 The Drone (1908) 26
 The Turn of the Road 25-6
Maze prison 57
McAuley, Maureen 188-9
McCabe, Lee 44
McCabe, Stanley 44
McCelland, Alan 76
McCracken, Henry Joy 49, 66, 119-21, 123, 124-135
McCracken, Kathleen 107

McCready, Sam 187
McDonagh, Martin
 Leenane Trilogy 202
McGuinness, Frank 206
 Observe the Sons of Ulster Marching Towards the Somme (1985) 66, 207
McElhinney, Ian 190, 203
McKee, Ritchie 42, 43-4
McKenna, Siobhán 44
McLarnon, Gerald 40
 The Bonfire (1958) 40
McPherson, Conor 202
McQuaid, Archbishop 42
Methven, Eleanor 188, 190
Meyer, Jean 197
Miami Showband 91-2, 99
Mitchell, Gary 14, 17, 46, 47, 157, 159-84, 206, 207, 208, 209
for television:
 An Officer from France (1998) 159
 As the Beast Sleeps (1998) 18, 159, 166, 176, 183
 Energy (2003/4) 159
 Falling (2005) 159
 Feud (2003/4) 159
 Made in Heaven (1996) 167
 Once Upon a Time in Belfast (2000/1)
 Red, White and Blue (1998) 159
 Sexton (2004) 159
 Suffering (2003) 159
 The Force of Change (2003/4) 159
for radio:
 As the Beast Sleeps (2001) 159, 166, 176
 Drumcree (1996) 159
 Independent Voice (1995) 160, 167
 Poison Hearts (1995) 159
 Stranded (1995) 159
 The World, the Flesh and the Devil (1991) 160, 161-2
for theatre:
 As the Beast Sleeps (1998) 160, 166, 176, 175-9
 Convictions: Holding Cell (2000) 160
 Deceptive Imperfections (2003) 160
 Dividing Force 163
 Energy (1999) 160

Force of Change 181
In a Little World of Our Own (1997) 18, 160, 162, 166, 167-74
  Loyal Women (2003) 160
  Marching On (2000) 18, 160, 180-3
  Remnants (2006) 160
  Sinking (1997) 160
  Something to Believe In (2005) 160
  Splinters (2003) 160
  State of Failure (2006) 160
  Tearing the Loom (1998) 18, 157, 160, 167, 172-4
  That Driving Ambition, Alternative Future, Exodus, Suspicious Mind, Independent Voice (1995) 160
  The Force of Change (2000) 160
  Trust (1999) 160, 167, 179-80
Molière 22
Moore, Thomas 72
Morrison, Bill 16, 206
Morrow, Harry C. (1865-1938) 23
  see also MacNamara, Gerald
Murphy, John
  The Country Boy (1959) 43
Murray, Christopher
  Twentieth Century Irish Drama: Mirror Up to Nature (1997) 206
Murray, Ruby 186

National Council of Labour Colleges (NCLC) 32
National Theatre, Belgium 77
New Ambassador Theatre, London 201
New Stage Club 16
New York Times 77
Nichol, Peter 85
Nolan, Brian 57
Northern Ireland Assembly 147, 148
Northern Ireland Labour Party 32, 191
Northern Star 123
Nowland, David 192
Nunn, Trevor 17

O'Casey, Sean 30, 47, 62, 63, 126, 127, 128, 135, 150, 208

The Drums of Father Ned (1958) 42
O'Callaghan, Maurice 43
O'Neill, Lord 31
O'Neill, Terence 41
Olivier Award 201
Olympia Theatre, Dublin 44
Orange Order 32, 122-3
Orangeism 23
Orangefield Girls' School 187
Osborne, John 48
  Look Back in Anger (1956) 41

Paisley, Reverend Ian 95
Papps, Joseph 64
Parades Commission 180
Parker, Stewart 13-17, 29, 30-1, 33, 35, 45-157, 159, 162, 163, 174, 185, 203, 205-9
Miscellaneous works:
  Bus Stories 53
  'Dramatis Personae' (1986) 16, 58, 68
  'High Pop' music column 56, 57
  John Malone Memorial Lecture 64, 112
  'Me and Jim' 16, 56
  'State of Play' 16
  'The Modern Poet as Dramatist' 53-4
for stage/radio/television:
  Catchpenny Twist (1977) 16, 71, 88-100, 102
  Deirdre Porter 75
  Heavenly Bodies 70
  Joyce in June 55
  Kingdom Come (1977) 16, 100-06
  Lost Belongings (1987) 16, 114-17
  Nightshade (1980) 16, 51, 106-10
  Pratt's Fall (1981) 16, 111-14
  Radio Pictures (1985) 55
  Spokesong 16, 46, 49, 57, 63, 65, 69, 71, 74-88, 91, 95, 100, 102, 105, 110, 112, 151
  The Iceberg (1974) 16, 55, 57-8, 65-6, 68-74, 85
  The Kamikaze Ground Staff Reunion Dinner (1981) 55
  Three Plays for Ireland 16-17, 48, 117, 119, 135, 136, 145, 146, 150

Heavenly Bodies (1986) 16, 120, 135-45

Northern Star (1984) 16, 49, 66, 70, 119-21, 123-35, 138, 172

Pentecost (1987) 16, 49, 117, 120, 135, 145-6, 149-55, 163

poetry:

The Casualty Meditates upon His Journey 53

Parkhill, David (1880-1941) 23

   The Enthusiast (1905) 24, 25

   The Reformers (1904) 24

Parnell, Charles Stewart 83

Parnellism 81

Peace Women 105

Peacock Theatre, Dublin 89, 162, 168, 171, 175, 192

Pearson Best Play of the Year Award 160

Pearson Television Theatre Writers' Scheme 163

Peters, Mary 76

Pig Marketing Board 56

Pike Theatre 41

Pinter, Harold 48

Plato

   Symposium 65

Playzone Theatre Group 188

Princess Theatre 138

Prix Europa 159

Purcell, Lewis, see Parkhill, David

Queen's University, Belfast 15, 45, 48, 52, 54, 76,156

Quigley, Peter 161

Quixote, Don 42

Rathcoole Secondary School 160-1

Rea, Stephen 76

Reid, Christina 206

Reid, Forrest (1875-1948) 24-5, 26

Reid, Graham 206

Riverside Studios, London 194

Robertson, Agnes 138

Robinson, Lennox 26

Roche, Anthony

   Contemporary Irish Drama, from Beckett to McGuinness (1995) 206

Rolston, Joan 187

Royal Court Theatre, London 76, 179

Royal National Theatre, London 163

Saint Brendan 111, 113

Scanlan, Carol 188, 190

Schechner, Richard 66

Scott, Sandy 76

Second World War 32, 187

Severin, Tim 111

Shan Van Vocht 121

Shaw, George Bernard 30, 127, 128, 134

   Heartbreak House 154

Shepherd, Sam 48

Sheridan, Peter 190, 191

Sheridan, Richard Brinsley 110, 128, 143

   The School for Scandal 142

Sidetracks, New York City 197

Silent Valley Reservoir 151

Simmons, James 52

Simpson, Alan 41-2

Sinn Féin (journal) 26

Social Democratic and Labour Party (SDLP) 147

Society of United Irishmen

   see United Irishmen

Socrates 65

Somme 66-7

Sony Award 159

South Bank Show Award 160

Square Theatre, New York 57, 77

Stembridge, Gerry

   Daisy the Cow Who Talked 203

Stewart Parker Award 160

Stoppard, Tom 48, 50

Stormont Parliament 150

Sullivan Upper School 15, 52

Sunningdale Agreement (1974) 147-8

Synge, John Millington 27, 30, 63, 107, 110, 120, 127, 128, 134

   The Playboy of the Western World 27, 113-14

The Northern Star 123
'The Voyage of Saint Brendan' 111
Theatre National, Brussels 77
Thompson, Sam 13, 14, 15, 29-37, 51, 57, 157, 162, 185, 203, 205, 208
BBC works:
  Brush in Hand (1956) 32
  The Fairmans (1959) 33
  The General Foreman (1958) 32
  The Long Back Street (1958) 33, 42
  Tommy Baxter - Shop Steward (1957) 32
  We Built a Ship (1959) 33
plays:
  Cemented with Love 45
  Over the Bridge 13, 15, 29-30, 31, 34-46, 66, 114, 162, 168, 205, 207-8
  The Evangelist (1963) 45, 46
  The Masquerade 45
Tinderbox Theatre Company 163
Titanic 67, 68, 69, 71-3
Tivoli Theatre, Dublin 201
Tomelty, Joseph 33
  The End House (1944) 41
  The McCooeys 33
Tone, Wolfe 23, 121, 122, 123, 133
Tricycle Theatre, London 197, 201
Tron Theatre, Glasgow 111
Troubles, the 55, 87, 90, 97
Tyrone Guthrie Centre 189

Ulster Defence Association (UDA) 160
Uladh 21-22, 23, 24, 26
Ulster Bridge Productions 44
Ulster Group Theatre 27, 42, 43, 188
Ulster Literary Theatre (ULT) 21, 22-7
Ulster Volunteer Force 91-2, 151
Ulster Workers' Strike (1974) 146, 150, 161
Unionist Party 32, 41, 147
United Irishmen 23, 119, 122-8, 131-2, 148
United Irishmen 24
United Ulster Unionist Council 147-8
Ustinov, Peter 77

Vestris, Madame 141
Vietnam War 119

Waddell, Sam (1878-1967) 23, 25
Weill, Kurt 58
West Belfast Festival 197
Wilde, Oscar 80, 110, 120, 127, 128, 132, 208
  The Importance of Being Earnest 130
Wilder, Thorton
  Our Town 85
Williams, Tennessee
  The Rose Tattoo (1951) 41-2
Winter, Brenda 189
Wilson, Harold 148, 149
Windsor Park, Belfast 197-9
Winter Garden Theatre 144
Women Mill Workers' Strike (1911) 189
World Cup 197
World War 1 66, 81, 82, 86

Yeats, W.B. 23, 24, 26, 54, 56, 63, 64, 70, 107, 110, 128
  Cathleen Ní Houlihan 23, 121
  Purgatory 70
  The Dreaming of the Bones 70
  The King's Threshold 24
  The Only Jealousy of Emer 70
  The Shadowy Waters 70
York Street Mill 189
Young, James 188
Young Playwrights Festival 160